Official Publisher Partnership

OCR
Citizenship Studies
Revision Guide
for GCSE short and full courses

Steve Johnson

CW00952405

HODDER EDUCATION
AN HACHETTE UK COMPANY

The Publishers would like to thank the following for permission to reproduce copyright material:
Photo credits: 12 © Hemmo1975/Dreamstime.com; 18 NMeM Daily Herald Archive; 28 © Hélène Plennevaux/International Committee of the Red Cross; 29 © Anthony Correia/Shutterstock.com; 32 © Metropolitan Police; 38 © Underwood & Underwood/CORBIS; 39t © fly/Shutterstock.com; 39b © Reuters/Corbis; 43 Rob Morgan March 2009 (www.flickr.com/photos/robtherunt); 49 © Sion Touhig/Corbis; 55 © Christophe Karaba/epa/Corbis; 78 © Dyson Ltd; 80 Triodos Bank; 82 Serco Ltd; 89 Fairtrade Foundation.

Acknowledgements: 45c Amnesty International; 45b RSPCA; 46 BBC (bbc.co.uk); 47, 64 BBC News (news.bbc.co.uk); 68 Crown Copyright; 71 BBC News (news.bbc.co.uk); 72 Local Government Ombudsman's Office; 74, 76 BBC News (news.bbc.co.uk); 78 Federation of Small Businesses (www.fsb.org.uk); 79 Mirrorpix (mirror.co.uk); 89 Fairtrade Foundation; 94 The Sun (thesun.co.uk); 95 Mirrorpix (mirror.co.uk); 96 BBC News (news.bbc.co.uk); 97 BBC World Service (www.bbc.co.uk/worldservice); 98 BBC (bbc.co.uk).

Every effort has been made to trace all copyright holders, but if any have been inadvertently overlooked the Publishers will be pleased to make the necessary arrangements at the first opportunity.

Although every effort has been made to ensure that website addresses are correct at time of going to press, Hodder Education cannot be held responsible for the content of any website mentioned in this book. It is sometimes possible to find a relocated web page by typing in the address of the home page for a website in the URL window of your browser.

Hachette UK's policy is to use papers that are natural, renewable and recyclable products and made from wood grown in sustainable forests. The logging and manufacturing processes are expected to conform to the environmental regulations of the country of origin.

Orders: please contact Bookpoint Ltd, 130 Milton Park, Abingdon, Oxon OX14 4SB. Telephone: (44) 01235 827720. Fax: (44) 01235 400454. Lines are open 9.00–5.00, Monday to Saturday, with a 24-hour message answering service. Visit our website at www.hoddereducation.co.uk.

© Steve Johnson 2009
First published in 2009 by
Hodder Education,
Carmelite House,
50 Victoria Embankment,
London EC4Y 0DZ.

Impression number   6
Year   2015

Produced for Hodder Education by White-Thomson Publishing Ltd. 0845 362 8240 www.wtpub.co.uk
Cover photos: *Protest* © Keith Reichner; *deforestation* © iStockphoto; policeman © Rudi Tapper/iStockphoto;
couple at market © Brand X/JupiterImages/Photolibrary.
Illustrations by Stefan Chabluk
Typeset in TheSans 10.5 pt by Andrew Solway
Text design: Big Blu Design
Printed and bound in Great Britain by Hobbs the Printers, Totton, Hants.

A catalogue record for this title is available from the British Library.

ISBN: 978 0340 99131 2
Student's Book ISBN: 978 0340 98249 5
Teacher's Resource Book ISBN: 978 0340 98282 2

Contents

Section 1 Introduction

Outline of the OCR Citizenship Studies specification   4
Guide to the short-course exam   6
Guide to the full-course exam   9

Section 2 Identity, democracy and justice: preparing for the short-course exam

2.1 Citizenship, identity and community in the United Kingdom   12
2.2 Fairness and justice in decision-making and the law   24
2.3 Democracy and voting   37
2.4 The United Kingdom and the wider world   51

Section 3 Rights and responsibilities: preparing for the full-course exam

3.1 Rights and responsibilities in school, college and the wider community 61
3.2 Rights and responsibilities as citizens within the economy and
    welfare systems   74
3.3 Extending our understanding of a global citizen's rights
    and responsibilities   85

Section 4 Answers to exam questions

Answers to questions from Section 2: short-course exam   99
Answers to questions from Section 3: full-course exam   102

Section 5 Glossary of key terms   107

Section 1 Introduction

Outline of the OCR Citizenship Studies specification

What are the aims and learning objectives?

The OCR specification is designed to help you prepare for your role as an informed and active citizen in your school, college and wider community.

By studying the short course (two units), you should learn the knowledge, understanding and skills defined in the national programme of study for Citizenship.

By studying the full course (four units), you will have the chance to broaden and deepen your knowledge, understanding and skills to help prepare you for a leading role as a citizen of the future.

The specification is designed to enable you to:
- Understand what it means to be British and the importance of community cohesion for the social and economic well-being of our society.
- Develop and apply the knowledge and understanding necessary to become an informed, active and responsible citizen on local, national and global scales.
- Advocate particular points of view based on evidence, while showing an understanding and respect for the views of others.
- Engage in your school, college and wider community as an active, responsible citizen.
- Research local, national and international issues and consider sustainable ways forward that are consistent with improving people's quality of life and respecting their human rights.

How is the specification organised?

The specification is organised into two themes (see diagram below):
1 'Rights and responsibilities', and
2 'Identity, democracy and justice'.

By studying the two short-course units, you should develop a reasonable understanding of each of these themes. By taking the two additional units of the full course, you should develop a very good understanding of both themes.

How the OCR Citizenship specification is organised.

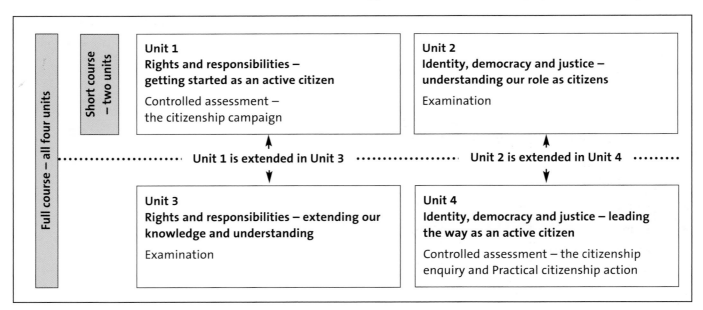

How does the assessment work?

Short course

You need to complete two units for the short-course certificate.

- Unit 1 Rights and responsibilities – getting started as an active citizen
- Unit 2 Identity, democracy and justice – understanding our role as citizens

Unit 1, on rights and responsibilities, is assessed through your planning, organisation and evaluation of a citizenship campaign. You will need to work with at least one other person on your campaign as you will be assessed partly on the effectiveness of your team-working and leadership skills. You will have a maximum of 37 hours to complete the assessment, which is worth 60 per cent of the overall short-course mark. Your teacher will guide you through the assessment.

Unit 2, on identity, democracy and justice, is assessed through a one-hour written examination. This book has been written to help you do well in this short-course exam.

Full course

If you would like a full-course certificate in Citizenship Studies, you complete two additional units.

- Unit 3 Rights and responsibilities – extending our knowledge and understanding
- Unit 4 Identity, democracy and justice – leading the way as an active citizen

Unit 3, on rights and responsibilities, is assessed through a one-hour written exam. This book will help you to do well in this full-course exam.

Unit 4, on identity, democracy and justice, is assessed through your research into a citizenship issue, and your planning, organisation and evaluation of some practical citizenship action. To help you with the citizenship issue, OCR provide a guide and selection of source material to get you started. You will need to work with at least one other person on your practical citizenship action, although your enquiry can take place independently. You will have a maximum of 37 hours to complete the assessment, which is worth 30 per cent of the overall full-course mark. Your teacher will guide you through the assessment.

How much is each assessment worth towards my final certificate?

The grid below shows how much each assessment element contributes towards the Citizenship Studies GCSE.

Units	Assessment activity	Short-course value	Full-course value
1	Citizenship campaign	60%	30%
2	Exam	40%	20%
3	Exam	–	20%
4	Citizenship enquiry and practical action	–	30%
Total		100%	100%

Guide to the short-course exam

Unit 2 Identity, democracy and justice – understanding our role as citizens

This one-hour exam is worth 40 per cent of the overall short-course mark, or 20 per cent of the full-course mark. The exam paper is marked out of a total of 40 marks.

The exam can be taken in January or June. The exam is also available as a computer-based test. You have the opportunity to re-take the short-course exam once if you wish to try to improve your mark.

Section A

Section A of the short-course exam contains the types of question below. You should spend approximately 30 minutes answering the questions in this section. There are 20 marks available.

Questions 1—5 are multiple-choice questions worth 1 mark each.

Example:
From the list below, select two reasons why law is important:
  i. Encouraging business.
  ii. Keeping order.
  iii. Sorting out problems.
  iv. Promoting cultural identity.

Questions 6—10 are short answer questions worth 1 mark each.

Example:
State one reason why migrants have recently come to live in the United Kingdom.

Question 11 is a short essay question worth 4 marks.

Example:
Explain why judges and juries are important in making sure that justice is done. In your answer you should:
- Explain why judges are important in making sure that justice is done.
- Explain why juries are important in making sure that justice is done.

Questions 12, 13 and 14 are based on statistical information presented in the form of tables, charts or maps. Question 14 is a short essay linked to the statistics, and is worth four marks.

Example of Question 14:
Explain why the United Nations gathers data on child health. In your answer you should:
- Describe the aims of the United Nations.
- Explain why problems with child health may get in the way of the United Nations achieving these aims.

Section B

Section B of the short-course exam contains two questions similar to the one below. You should answer both questions in approximately 10 minutes.

For questions 15 and 16 you will need to read a short story about a young person and, using your understanding of the law, decide between three alternatives. You will also have to describe their rights or responsibilities. Each question is worth 4 marks.

Example:
Read Document 1 below. Study each of the alternatives i—iii.

Document 1

Joe is 19 and has been arrested. He is so confused that he is not clear about what is going on. Joe just wants to get it all over with and go home. What should he do?
  i. Joe should stop worrying as he can definitely return home in 8 hours.
  ii. Joe should ask for the duty solicitor.
  iii. Joe must answer the questions asked by the police.

Evaluate this case. In your answer you should:
- Select one of the alternatives (i, ii or iii above) to show what Joe should do.
- Explain why you have chosen this alternative.
- Explain Joe's rights or responsibilities in this case.

Section C

Section C of the short-course exam contains one essay question similar to the one below. You should spend approximately 20 minutes on this question.

Question 17 is an essay question worth 12 marks out of the 40 available for the paper.

Example:
Evaluate the following viewpoint: 'The most important organisation in the legal and justice system is the police.' In your answer, you should:
- Evaluate the importance of the police's role in the legal and justice system.
- Evaluate the importance of the parts played by other groups and organisations.
- Use evidence or examples to support your points.
- Sum up your response to the viewpoint.

Revising for the short-course exam (Identity, democracy and justice)

You should revise for the short-course exam using the checklist that follows. Some notes have been included for the first section. These should help you to remember the main points in preparation for your exam.

Short-course checklist

Citizenship, identity and community in the United Kingdom (see pp 12–23)

I can ... (tick box when confident)

- ❏ Describe the cultural traditions that contribute to being British. *(Make sure you can describe at least two of these.)*

- ❏ Describe the main values that contribute to being British. *(These are democracy, equal opportunity, freedom, the rule of law and fair play.)*

- ❏ Describe the nations of the UK. *(England, Scotland, Wales and Northern Ireland.)*

- ❏ Describe the different regions of England or Wales. *(Make sure you know at least three.)*

- ❏ Describe the main ethnic groups in the UK. *(The main ethnic groups are White British, Indian, Pakistani, Bangladeshi, Caribbean and African with many recent immigrants from eastern Europe.)*

- ❏ Describe the main religious groups in the UK. *(Christian, Muslim, Sikh, Jew and Hindu.)*

- ❏ Explain why people migrate from one place to another. *(Think of examples of push factors and pull factors.)*

- ❏ Explain why people seek asylum. *(Seeking asylum is asking permission to stay in the country you have moved to because it is not safe to stay in your own country.)*

- ❏ Explain why the UK is a country with wide cultural diversity. *(Migration to the UK from the British Commonwealth, Afghanistan, Iraq, Iran, parts of North Africa, North America, Australia, New Zealand and European countries.)*

- ❏ Explain why people's sense of identity is often complex. *(Someone whose parents were born in another country may have to choose between following their friends' traditions and behaviour, and those of their parents.)*

- ❏ Describe how people of different ethnic origins and religious backgrounds contribute to the national economy. *(Consider examples from business, politics, sport and entertainment.)*

- ❏ Explain what is meant by the term community cohesion. *(Community cohesion is where people in a community feel a sense of belonging. They support one another and get on well. Where community cohesion is strong, there are low levels of crime, vandalism and racism.)*

Short-course checklist (continued)

Fairness and justice in decision-making and the law (see pp 24–36)

I can ...

- ❑ Describe how the police, the Crown Prosecution Service (CPS) and criminal courts uphold the law and deal with criminals.
- ❑ Explain why crime can threaten human rights.
- ❑ Describe how human rights are protected by the Universal Declaration of Human Rights, the Human Rights Act and international humanitarian law.
- ❑ Describe how rights can compete and conflict.
- ❑ Explain how the law can help where rights compete or conflict.
- ❑ Describe the responsibilities a citizen has to obey the law and support the justice system.
- ❑ Describe the rights a citizen has if stopped or arrested by the police.
- ❑ Describe how a Bill passes through the UK Parliament to become an Act and new law.
- ❑ Describe how legal advice and support may be obtained.

Democracy and voting (see pp 37–50)

I can ...

- ❑ Understand the different operation of power and authority in democratic and non-democratic forms of government, historically and across the world today. *(In a democracy there are regular elections and secret voting. There are different political parties to choose from. The media can comment freely and citizens have free speech. Human rights are respected and politicians have to obey the law. With a non-democratic government people have fewer rights, cannot vote and the media is government-controlled.)*
- ❑ Explain why non-democratic forms of government are likely to infringe on human rights.
- ❑ Explain the term 'representative democracy'.

- ❑ Explain Parliament's role in making the Government accountable.
- ❑ Describe how citizens can play an active part in local and national elections.
- ❑ Describe how citizens can influence decision-making by joining political parties.
- ❑ Describe how citizens can influence decision-making by joining pressure groups or religious organisations.
- ❑ Describe how the media influences public debate and decision-making.
- ❑ Describe how citizens and politicians can make use of the media.
- ❑ Evaluate how far citizens are able to hold decision-makers to account.
- ❑ Explain why a free press is important in a democracy.

The UK's relationships in Europe, including the EU, the Commonwealth and UN (see pp 51–60)

I can ...

- ❑ Describe, in outline, the UK's cultural relationships with Europe.
- ❑ Describe, in outline, the UK's economic relationships with Europe.
- ❑ Describe, in outline, the UK's political and legal relationships with Europe.
- ❑ Describe how European Union (EU) decisions have an impact upon citizens of the UK.
- ❑ Evaluate the benefits and costs of the UK's membership of the EU.
- ❑ Explain that the British Commonwealth is a family of nations and has an important role in promoting cultural understanding and the exchange of ideas.
- ❑ Describe the United Nations' (UN's) role in helping to resolve international conflict.
- ❑ Explain why the UK has agreed to follow the UN's agreements on human rights, international relations and the environment.
- ❑ Describe the role and effectiveness of the UN in one international issue, emergency or dispute.

Guide to the full-course exam

Unit 3 Rights and responsibilities – extending our knowledge and understanding

This one-hour exam is worth 20 per cent of the overall full-course mark. The exam paper is marked out of a total of 40 marks.

The exam can be taken only in June. You have the opportunity to re-take the full-course exam once if you wish to try to improve your mark.

Section A

Section A of the full-course exam contains the types of question below. You should answer all the questions in approximately 25 minutes. There are 18 marks available in this section.

Questions 1a–5b are short-answer questions usually worth 1 mark each. (There are 12 marks in total for these questions.)

Example:
State one way in which a trade union supports its members.

Question 6 is an essay question worth 6 marks.

Example:
Explain how Student or School Councils can help to promote rights and responsibilities in a school or college. In your answer, you must:
- Explain in depth one way in which Student or School Councils promote rights and responsibilities, or explain, in outline, at least two ways in which this is done.
- Use examples to support your explanation.

Section B

Section B of the full-course exam contains the types of question in the examples below. You should answer all the questions in approximately 35 minutes. There are 22 marks available in this section.

Each question in this section is linked to stimulus documents that you should read very carefully. You should use information from the stimulus documents to help you answer the questions, as well as your own knowledge, understanding and experience of Citizenship Studies.

Questions 7, 8 and 9 contain a mix of tasks – some will need a short answer and others a more detailed response. Each question is based on at least one stimulus document. You must answer three such questions. Altogether they are worth 22 marks.

Example:
In April 2009 the National Union of Teachers (NUT) threatened to boycott (not do) the standard assessment tasks (SATs) in primary schools. They were told by the Government that if they went ahead with the threat, they would be breaking the law.

Study Documents 1 to 3, then answer the questions that follow.

Document 1
Adapted from the BBC website (www.bbc.co.uk)

Hazel Danson, a member of the NUT executive, said testing did not raise standards, but damaged children's learning.

Max Hyde, supporting her, said SATs must end. 'They are damaging and distort the curriculum and, especially for the most vulnerable children, they are close to a form of child abuse.'

David Clinch, a teacher from Devon, said: 'SATs are like cigarettes. They've got no benefit to the human body whatsoever. What they do is make children very nervous about their learning. In fact they are not learning, they are being coached to do particular tests which have no benefit to them at all. The key benefit of SATs is for the Government to make schools compete against one another and to put schools into league tables.'

Document 2
Adapted from the BBC website (www.bbc.co.uk)

A spokeswoman for the Education Department said: 'I regret that the NUT are going against the clear wishes of parents and the need to raise standards in every school and in every child. This boycott is unlawful and will cause great disruption to the schools. It also sends the wrong message to young people and harms teachers' reputations.

'The unions representing the majority of teachers do not support the approach of the NUT leadership and we call on the NUT to think again.'

The other unions that represent teachers have not backed the campaign.

Document 3

Adapted from the website of the National Governors' Association (www.nga.org.uk)

The primary school SATs do not tell teachers and parents enough about an individual child's progress. They have led to a system of test cramming for ten-year-old children in too many schools. The NGA believes this is unacceptable.

For these reasons the NGA is opposed to league tables. However, the NGA also believes that parents have a right to know how their child's school is performing.

i. State one argument in favour of the SATs ending from Document 1. *(1 mark)*

ii. State one reason from Document 2 for the Government being against the NUT boycott of SATs. *(1 mark)*

iii. State one point from the NGA in Document 3 that agrees with the NUT viewpoint on SATs. *(1 mark)*

iv. Evaluate the viewpoint that the NUT was right to threaten to boycott SATs in primary schools. In your answer you must do the following.
- Explain arguments in favour of the boycott.
- Explain arguments against the boycott.
- Explain whether a trade union should boycott something the Government has introduced.
- Explain your own point of view on the threatened boycott. *(6 marks)*

Revising for the full-course exam (Rights and responsibilities)

You should revise for the full-course exam using the checklist in the next column. This follows the same format as revision for the short-course exam. Again, some notes have been included in the first section.

Use Section 3 of this revision book to help you complete your revision notes.

Full-course checklist

Rights and responsibilities in school, college and the wider community (see pp 61–73)

I can … (tick box when confident)

☐ Describe the moral rights people have at school or college. *(These include students having the right to learn and teachers having the right to teach.)*

☐ Describe the moral responsibilities people have at school or college. *(Moral responsibilities for students include completing and handing in work on time. For teachers, moral responsibilities include assessing students' work clearly and handing it back promptly.)*

☐ Describe the legal rights people have at school or college. *(Legal rights for students include studying the National Curriculum and learning in a safe environment. Legal rights for teachers include being able to punish students by giving them detentions.)*

☐ Describe the legal responsibilities people have at school or college. *(Legal responsibilities of teachers include reporting students' progress to their parents or carers at least once a year. Legal responsibilities of parents include making sure their children receive a suitable education by sending them to school or by arranging some other method of education.)*

☐ Explain how legal rights and responsibilities are reinforced and protected in schools. *(Legal rights and responsibilities are reinforced and protected by such things as a complaints process for parents, school policies setting out expectations clearly, elected governors and a regular inspection process.)*

☐ Evaluate how effective local authorities or government departments are at giving advice and support to citizens about their rights. *(Local authorities vary in how good they are about giving advice and support to citizens regarding their rights. Make sure you have checked on the effectiveness of at least one local authority. Government departments are usually good at giving advice and support. There are clear websites, help lines and facilities for people with disabilities or for whom English is an additional language. Make sure that you have evaluated the website of at least one government department.)*

❑ Evaluate how effective independent agencies are at providing citizens with information and advice about their rights. *(Independent agencies are good at providing citizens with information and advice about their rights. Youth organisations have websites designed for young people's needs. Make sure you have checked on the effectiveness of at least one such website and can give examples of the type and usefulness of the advice provided.)*

❑ Describe some of the human rights protected by the Universal Declaration of Human Rights, the European Convention on Human Rights and the Human Rights Act. *(Some of the main rights protected by the above are rights to life, liberty, security, a fair trial, be a candidate in an election, vote, think and speak freely, meet with others and be able to own property.)*

❑ Evaluate how effective the Universal Declaration of Human Rights is at protecting human rights across the world. *(The United Nations Universal Declaration of Human Rights has had a considerable influence on laws across Europe and in the United Kingdom. People's rights enjoy a considerable level of protection as a result of the Universal Declaration. However, even in the UK, there are claims that people's human rights are restricted unreasonably because of fear of terrorism. In non-democratic countries such as North Korea, people have considerable problems in speaking freely, getting a fair trial and standing for election.)*

Rights and responsibilities as citizens within the economy and welfare systems (see pp 74–84)

I can …

❑ Explain why the interests of employers and employees can conflict.

❑ Describe how the law protects the interests of employers and employees.

❑ Explain how employers' interests might conflict with the need to protect the environment.

❑ Describe how the Government uses taxation and regulation to encourage environmentally responsible behaviour.

❑ Describe how trade unions support and represent their members.

❑ Describe how employers' associations support and represent their members.

❑ Explain why patent law and copyright law are important for business.

❑ Explain why it is important for businesses to be socially responsible.

❑ Describe how the Government helps to manage the economy.

❑ Describe the public services that are provided by the Government and local authorities.

❑ Evaluate how much responsibility the state or individuals should have for the provision of income protection, health and education.

Extending our understanding of a global citizen's rights and responsibilities (see pp 85–98)

I can …

❑ Describe how sustainable development is promoted locally.

❑ Describe how sustainable development is promoted nationally.

❑ Describe how sustainable development is promoted globally.

❑ Describe the features of fair trade.

❑ Describe how governments can encourage fairer trade.

❑ Explain why More Economically Developed Countries (MEDCs) should give aid to Less Economically Developed Countries (LEDCs).

❑ Evaluate different types of overseas aid.

❑ Describe how the media affects public opinion.

❑ Describe how the media can help bring about change in democratic societies.

❑ Describe how the media can help bring about change in non-democratic societies.

2.1 Citizenship, identity and community in the United Kingdom

What are the cultural traditions that contribute to being British?

The United Kingdom (UK) is a multicultural society. Groups of people from all over the world have come to settle in the UK, bringing their cultural traditions with them. Some of these traditions have been widely adopted across the UK. Here are two examples.

- Settlers from the Caribbean brought their tradition of street carnivals to London. The Notting Hill Carnival is now one of the biggest carnivals in the world and is enjoyed in late August each year by tens of thousands of people from different backgrounds.
- Immigrants from India and Pakistan brought their tradition for hot, spicy food that had already been popular with the British in India for 200 years. Now there is a curry house in every town and some villages in the UK.

There are many other cultural traditions in Britain that people take for granted, but miss if they go to live in another country. Examples include school uniforms, Remembrance Sunday, Mothers' Day and the English pub. These traditions are often linked to the UK's official Protestant religion or to the country's history.

People across the UK are passionate about certain sports. Rugby and football are two examples. For the English, cricket is a traditional summer sport enjoyed by many. Horse racing, show jumping, motor racing, boxing, rowing and sailing are also sports that are seen as British specialities. The UK is also well known for the quality of its education, music, theatre, film and television.

As the home of the English language, the UK remains a place in which many people across the world are interested. Our culture is seen as rich and traditional but increasingly varied as new cultural traditions become established across the country.

What are the main values that contribute to being British?

Values are the moral principles or accepted standards held by an individual or group of people. To find out what official British values are, we should study the rules that govern the actions of public bodies connected with the law, justice, communication and education. These rules are usually based on the following core values.

The rule of law

The rule of law means that the law applies to everyone, even politicians, judges, the police and the very wealthy.

> ### Key terms
>
> **Values** Beliefs or principles that we hold to be important.

🔺 **Justice is blind. It doesn't matter who you are, the law applies to you.**

Personal freedom

People should be free to benefit from their hard work, travel freely, and say and write what they like as long as it does not harm others. Businesses should be free to run their organisations without undue interference from the government. Artists, playwrights, designers, authors and musicians should be free to take risks and try new things. Everyone can criticise the government, put forward new ideas and make fun of celebrities, politicians, business people and even religious leaders.

Tolerance and respect for diversity

Tolerance and respect for diversity are linked to personal freedom. The UK has built up an international reputation for accepting people of different religious faiths and cultural traditions. In the last 300 years many people have come to the UK to escape mistreatment in their home country.

Equal opportunity

Equal opportunity means that everyone should have the same chances to achieve their ambitions as everyone else. Women should have the same chances as men. It shouldn't matter about your race, culture, religion or age. What should count is your ability and experience.

Representative democracy

One of the main values in the UK is that everyone has a right to a say in how the country is run. Elections are fair and each person's vote is a secret. For more on representative democracy, see pages 41–42.

> ### Key terms
>
> **Parliament** The main law-making body of the United Kingdom, consisting of the House of Commons, the House of Lords and the Crown (the king or queen).

The United Kingdom is made up of four nations: England, Scotland, Wales and Northern Ireland.

Northern Ireland Until recently Northern Ireland was bitterly divided between loyalists (people who want to remain part of the UK) and republicans (people who want Northern Ireland to leave the UK). The two sides now share power in the Northern Ireland Assembly with responsibility for education, planning and development and public safety. The assembly can pass its own laws.

Wales An independent country until 1543, Wales has its own language. This almost died out in the 1960s but is now becoming more popular. The Welsh Assembly, formed in 1998, has responsibility for planning and the development of the environment, culture and sport as well as aspects of education, health and transport. The assembly cannot pass its own laws but can make important changes to the ways in which UK laws apply in Wales.

Scotland An independent country until 1707, Scotland has its own parliament with the power to pass its own laws. Scotland's legal system is separate from the rest of the United Kingdom. In 2009, the Scottish Nationalist Party held power in the Scottish Parliament and many were predicting that Scotland might break away from the rest of the UK.

England England does not have its own assembly. Everything that affects England is decided through the United Kingdom **Parliament**. In addition, the UK Parliament makes decisions about systems of government, taxation, economic policy and defence for the whole of the UK.

What are the different regions of England and Wales?

England and Wales are both small countries in comparison to most countries in the world. Nevertheless, both England and Wales have a wide variety of landscapes, including mountain ranges and large rivers. Both countries also have considerable variations in climate, ranging from the west of Wales with its mild, wet climate to East Anglia where it is dry as well as being very warm in summer and cold in winter. In the past, these physical features and differences in climate helped to divide the English and Welsh people into regions, such as East Anglia or North Wales, with their own types of occupation, culture and, until the start of the nineteenth century, different time zones.

The regions themselves are divided into counties that have traditionally acted as the areas for local government in England and Wales. There are still fierce rivalries between counties. One of the most passionate rivalries is between the counties of Yorkshire and Lancashire. This has its origins in a civil war known as the Wars of the Roses (1453–1487).

Many people are intensely proud about which part of England or Wales they are from. They celebrate regional and county differences in food, drink, breeds of animal and allegiance to particular football, rugby or cricket teams.

What are the main ethnic groups in England and Wales?

An ethnic group is a group of people who identify with one another through a shared cultural heritage often based on their upbringing, country of origin or religion. Sixteen per cent of the population of England and Wales belongs to an ethnic minority group. Although most

Table A. Ethnic groups in England, 2006
(Adapted from data from the Government Statistical Office, 2008)

Ethnic group	% of the total population
White British	86.0
Indian, Pakistani, Bangladeshi or other Asian	5.4
White Irish or other white background	4.5
Black Caribbean	1.2
Black African or other black background	1.6
Chinese	0.7
Other ethnic background	0.7
Mixed ethnic background*	1.6

*There are nearly one million people in England with a mixed ethnic background. This may be because one of their parents is White British and the other is Asian. As people from different cultures mix more easily, there are likely to be more people from a mixed ethnic background in the future. See also page 20.

are born in Britain, their parents, grandparents or great grandparents may have been born overseas.

What are the main religious groups in England and Wales?

The 2001 National Census collected information about all the people living in England and Wales at that time. Part of this information was about ethnicity and religious identity. The results show that it is a mistake to think that all people from a particular ethnic group follow the same religion. However, while there is a great variety of ethnic and religious groups, white Christians remain the largest single group by far.

- In England and Wales, 36 million people (nearly seven out of ten) described their ethnicity as white and their religion as Christian.
- The majority of black people (71 per cent) and those from mixed backgrounds (52 per cent) also identified themselves as Christian.
- Among other faiths the largest groups were Pakistani Muslims and Indian Hindus, followed by Indian Sikhs, Bangladeshi Muslims and white Jews.
- The Indian ethnic group was religiously diverse: 45 per cent of Indians were Hindu, 29 per cent Sikh and a further 13 per cent Muslim. In contrast the Pakistani and Bangladeshi groups largely followed Islam – 92 per cent of each ethnic group were Muslim.
- Some religions were linked to particular ethnic groups. For example, 91 per cent of Sikhs were Indian and 97 per cent of Jews described their ethnicity as white. Other religions were more widely spread. For example, considerable proportions of Buddhists were found to belong to white, Chinese or Asian ethnic groups.

Overall, 15 per cent of the English and Welsh population reported having no religion, although there was considerable variation by ethnic group. Just over half of all Chinese people and one quarter of people from mixed ethnic backgrounds stated they had no religion. Asian, black African and white Irish people were least likely to have no religion. Fewer than 1 in 200 Pakistanis and Bangladeshis reported having no religion.

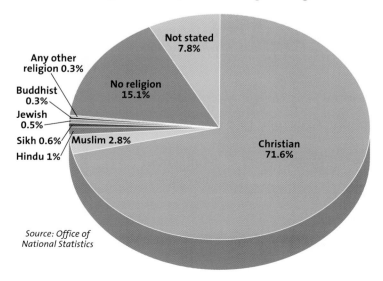

Source: Office of
National Statistics

Not stated
7.8%

Any other
religion 0.3%

Buddhist
0.3%

No religion
15.1%

Jewish
0.5%

Sikh 0.6% Muslim 2.8%

Hindu 1%

Christian
71.6%

◐ The 2001 National Census asked people about their religious beliefs, if they had them. This pie chart summarises the results.

Why do people migrate from one place to another?

The movement of people (migration) from one place to another is normal. Try some research on your own family or one that you know. Where do grandparents, aunts, uncles and cousins live? Have they always lived in the same place? What were their reasons for moving? The family tree below helps to tell one family's story.

Grandparents

Archie Born in Aberdeen, Scotland. Met Susan on holiday in Wales. Moved to Birmingham to be close to Susan's family. Now retired to Scarborough, Yorkshire.

Susan Born in Birmingham. Lived there all her life but now retired to Scarborough with Archie.

Marlon Born in Jamaica but moved to Florida to get a better job. Met Kate in Florida, moved to London with her and became a British citizen.

Kate Born in Germany where parents were based (father in the army). Moved back to London but spent time working in the USA, where she met Marlon.

Parents

Tom Born in Birmingham but moved to London to go to college. Now a self-employed plumber in Brighton, where the family moved because housing was cheaper than in London.

Rose Met Tom in Spain, where she was working for a travel company. Now works in a bank in Brighton. She has a sister who emigrated to Canada with her family.

Children

Archie Went to university in Edinburgh. Now works in China teaching English.

Alicia At college in Scarborough where she lives with her grandparents to keep costs down.

Beatrice On a gap year in Australia. Now has a boyfriend over there and may decide to stay.

PUSH FACTORS – reasons why people might emigrate (leave their home).

- Fear for their lives (war or terrorism)
- Fear for their lives (natural disasters)
- Discrimination
- No work or poorly paid work
- Famine
- Disease or pollution
- Lack of educational opportunities
- High cost of living

→ **Emigration** (moving out)

PULL FACTORS – reasons why other places might attract people (immigration).

- Peaceful place
- Good record of human rights
- Employment available
- High standard of living
- Other members of their family or ethnic group live there
- Good health care and education

← **Immigration** (moving in)

Why do people seek asylum in the UK?

What is asylum?

When people ask for asylum, they are asking for refuge or protection. A person seeking refuge is known as a refugee. Refugees feel unable to return to their home country. They have a realistic fear that they or members of their family may be killed, injured, tortured, imprisoned or subjected to unreasonable discrimination. Asylum is given under the 1951 United Nations Convention Relating to the Status of Refugees.

The UK has a proud record of providing a home for people who have had to leave their own country because their lives are threatened or because they are being discriminated against. The first refugees were from Europe, but more recently refugees have come to the UK from South America, Asia and Africa.

The number of people seeking asylum without good reason has increased in recent years. As a result, the UK Government refuses protection to those who do not need it and removes **asylum seekers** who have made false claims. However, the UK follows the European Convention on Human Rights, and so should not send an asylum seekers to a country where there is a real risk they will be exposed to torture or inhuman or degrading treatment or punishment.

Why do people seek asylum in the UK?

People seek refuge in the UK for various reasons:

- The UK has a good record on human rights – see also British values on pages 12 to 13.
- English is spoken across the world and is a familiar language, so many people prefer to live in an English-speaking country.
- People belonging to the asylum-seeker's ethnic group may already live somewhere in the UK.
- The UK is a wealthy country that can afford to support asylum seekers.
- Between 1996 and 2007 jobs were widely available in the UK. Many of these jobs were unskilled and it was not necessary for the people doing them to speak good English.
- People who live in the UK have a right to housing, education and health care.

In 2007, nineteen out of every hundred people who applied for asylum were recognised as refugees and given asylum. Another nine in every hundred, who applied for asylum but did not qualify for refugee status, were given permission to stay for humanitarian or other reasons. (At the time these figures were published, seventeen in every hundred applications had not yet resulted in a final decision.)

The **UK Border Agency** sets out the following rights and responsibilities for people claiming asylum in the UK (see overleaf).

Asylum seekers' rights

- To be treated fairly and lawfully regardless of your race, gender, age, religion, sexual orientation or any disability.
- To practise your own religion (you are expected to respect people of other faiths).
- To have your application considered fairly and accurately.
- To have access to support and housing if you meet the requirements for it.
- To have access to free health care from the National Health Service (NHS).
- To have legal representation. (Free legal help may be available, depending on income and circumstances.)

Asylum seekers' responsibilities

- To co-operate with the UK Border Agency and tell the truth. (It is a crime to make a false asylum application. A false claim could lead to imprisonment and deportation).
- To stay in regular contact with the UK Border Agency and keep all your appointments.
- To obey the law.
- To care for your children. (An adult must always supervise children under the age of sixteen, and if they are aged between five and sixteen they must have full-time education, usually at school.)
- To leave the United Kingdom if your application is refused.

Why does the UK have such wide cultural diversity?

London – an international city

There are very few cities in the world where you can order breakfast in Farsi, book a taxi in Urdu, ask for afternoon coffee in Arabic and spend the evening chatting in Cantonese. But all of this can be done in London.

There are 300 different languages regularly spoken in London. This is many more than any other European city. Only New York has a similar level of diversity. Such diversity has many benefits. The range of languages spoken in London is a major attraction for companies operating within the global market. For example, Air France has its global reservation centre in Wembley, north-west London, rather than in Paris. Other airlines have made a similar choice.

Key terms

Immigrant A person who has left from their home region or country and is living in another region or country.

The ship *SS Empire Windrush* brought one of the first groups of **immigrants** to the UK from the Caribbean. They filled some of the vacant jobs in London after the Second World War.

London's range of languages matches the ethnic mix in the city. London is home to many communities of people who were born outside England. There are 33 ethnic communities in London numbering more than 10,000 people. They range from those born in Ireland, who number more than 200,000, to the Mauritian community, which numbers around 14,000. A further 12 communities include more than 5,000 people.

The United Kingdom – a culturally diverse nation

The United Kingdom, like its capital city, is becoming increasingly culturally diverse. Many people who come from overseas to make their home in London, later move on to live outside the capital. Immigrants have settled widely across the UK in cities such as Edinburgh, Glasgow, Cardiff, Leeds, Manchester, Liverpool, Hull, Bristol, Birmingham and Southampton. More recently, agricultural workers from Europe have moved into rural areas of the UK such as south-west England, East Anglia and Lincolnshire.

Cultural diversity explained

History helps explain the reasons for the United Kingdom's cultural diversity. The UK has been a great trading nation for many hundreds of years. During the 1700s and early 1800s, much of this trade involved the buying and selling of slaves. Ships from Bristol and Liverpool carried cargoes of people from Africa to the Caribbean and the USA. One result of this trade was the growth, over 200 years ago, of small black communities in Bristol, Cardiff and Liverpool. At the same time, refugees from Europe came to the UK to settle in cities such as London, Hull and Norwich.

During the 1700 and 1800s the UK was **colonising** land all across the world to increase trade and prosperity. The Indian subcontinent, large parts of Africa, most of the Caribbean and even parts of Asia were under British control by the end of the 1800s. People across the British **Empire** were encouraged to see Queen Victoria as their queen, to learn English and to see the world from a British point of view. Many people in these countries were given the right to have a British passport and the right to live in the UK if they wished.

During the twentieth century, most of these British colonies gained their independence and joined the British Commonwealth (see page 56). When additional workers were needed in the UK after the Second World War it was natural to recruit labour from these former British territories. People were keen to start a new life in what many regarded as their 'mother country'. Large numbers of immigrants arrived in the UK from British Commonwealth countries from 1950 through to 1990.

More recently, more people have asked for asylum (a safe refuge) in the UK than at any other time in our history. Free movement of workers within the European Union (see page 55) has meant that many EU citizens, particularly from eastern Europe and France, have settled in the UK.

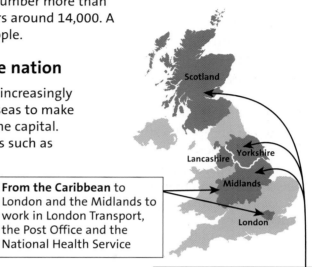

⬇ Map showing the main areas of the UK where immigrants settled, 1950–1990.

From the Caribbean to London and the Midlands to work in London Transport, the Post Office and the National Health Service

From the Indian subcontinent to work in the cotton and woollen mills of Lancashire and Yorkshire and factories in the Midlands and Scotland

Key terms

Colonising Conquering and taking over control of a region or country.

Empire A group of countries under the rule of a single person or state. In the British Empire, for example, Canada, India and large parts of Africa were ruled from London.

As unemployment increased in the UK during 2009, immigration was reduced. The Government made it harder for immigrants from outside the EU to move to the UK and there were fewer jobs to attract newcomers.

Why do people in the UK often have a complex sense of identity?

We develop our sense of who we are (our identity) from a number of different sources. When we are very young, we spend most time with our parents and learn from them. Parents shape our values, habits and behaviour. We follow their cultural traditions without question.

As we get older, we mix with a wider variety of people. This first happens at school and then at college or university and at work. Our friends may have different values, habits and behaviour from our parents, relatives and members of our community. Reading, watching TV, listening to music, travelling or just shopping gives us access to new ideas and ways of behaving. The UK is a very diverse society with plenty of choices for us to make as we develop our sense of identity. As we do so, we may begin to question the values and traditions of our parents and move away from the cultural ties that were so important when we were younger.

People who belong to a minority ethnic group have to balance the values, culture and traditions of that ethnic group against the expectations people have of all young people in the UK. This is usally not a problem. Most people who are part of an ethnic minority group can also celebrate their Britishness. However, there can be difficulties if the expectations of the ethnic group are very different from those of other people in the UK. For example, some Muslim girls have serious disputes with their parents about what is appropriate behaviour with boyfriends.

All this can make for a complex sense of identity. Personal identity can sometimes be even more complex for the nearly one million people in England with a mixed ethnic background.

What contributes to our sense of identity?

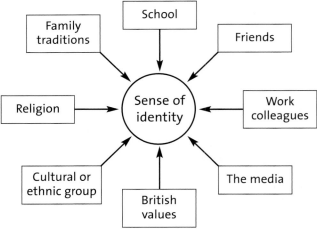

Table B. Numbers of UK citizens belonging to mixed ethnic groups

Ethnic group of UK citizens, 2006	Number
Mixed white and black Caribbean	274,000
Mixed white and black African	108,000
Mixed white and Asian	264,000
Other mixed ethnic groups	201,000

How much do people of different ethnic origins and religious backgrounds contribute to the national economy?

People from a wide range of ethnic and religious backgrounds now contribute very substantially to the national economy and to the success of the UK as a nation.

Remember that in the 1950s, 60s, 70s and 80s many immigrants from the Caribbean, Africa and Asia came to the UK to do low-skilled and poorly paid jobs. They also faced widespread racism and discrimination.

Even though racial discrimination became illegal in 1976, people from ethnic minority groups still found it difficult to break out of poverty. However, as the UK has become a much more diverse society and racism has become unacceptable, it has been easier for people from ethnic minority groups to achieve success. While many children from ethnic minority groups have problems to overcome, especially at school, others have achieved very prominent positions in business, politics, the media, sport and entertainment. Three examples of the many ethnic minority success stories are given below.

Shaf Rasul

Shaf Rasul is Scotland's richest Asian, with a personal fortune of more than £100 million. The 37-year-old has made his millions in property and computers. He established his optical-media distribution company, E-Net Computers Limited, in 2000 and expanded to become the largest storage media distributor in Europe.

At the same time he had investments in property and business worth nearly £30 million. In 2009 Raul joined the popular BBC TV programme *Dragon's Den* to assess the ideas of up-and-coming business people.

Munira Mirza

Munira Mirza was born in the UK. Her parents are from Pakistan. Munira Mirza is a graduate of Oxford University and is the Mayor of London's director of arts and cultural policy. A writer and broadcaster on race and cultural issues, Munira Mirza designed a month-long celebration of London's past, present and future in June 2009. She also has a number of innovative plans in the pipeline such as a Culture Pass for young people.

Kelly Holmes

Kelly Holmes was born in the UK in 1970. Her father is Jamaican and her mother is English. At eighteen she joined the army, where she drove four-tonne trucks. She later retrained as an army physical training instructor. She became army judo champion, ran in the men's 1500 m race at the army athletics championships, and in one meeting ran the 800 m, the 3000 m and a relay leg in one day, winning all three races.

In 2004 she won double Olympic gold (800 and 1500 m) at the Athens Olympics and was given the title Dame Kelly Holmes. She was also the 2004 BBC Sports Personality of the Year. Dame Kelly is now a writer and broadcaster.

What is community cohesion?

Community cohesion means people sharing values and goals and living together well.

Things you might find in a neighbourhood with high levels of community cohesion:

- People of all ages out on the streets without fear.
- Tidy streets, gardens, parks and public areas.
- Houses and flats lived in and cared for.
- People mixing in shops, cafes and parks.
- Successful schools, libraries and community centres with lots of services for the whole community.
- Low levels of discrimination and racism.

Things you might find in a neighbourhood with low levels of community cohesion:

- People afraid to leave their homes, especially at night.
- Vandalism, graffiti and litter.
- Houses and flats empty.
- People going to particular shops and cafes to avoid other groups.
- Failing schools with little provision for the community.
- High levels of discrimination and racism.

Recently the British Government has become concerned about the lack of community cohesion in the UK.

Some people from ethnic minority groups gain most of their identity and sense of community from their family, neighbourhood and religious group rather than seeing themselves as British citizens. Discrimination and racism have made many feel excluded and have helped to create a country in which our schools and communities are often divided by ethnicity and religion. Trevor Phillips, chairman of the Equality and Human Rights Commission, has warned that we are 'sleepwalking towards segregation' and 'becoming strangers to each other'. He is worried that ethnic and religious groups lead separate lives in their own schools and neighbourhoods.

It is natural for groups of people who first arrive in a new country to stick together and maintain their own family, cultural and religious traditions. However, the separation of one group from another has had many negative consequences for the UK, including educational underachievement and violence between different ethnic groups. Similar problems have occurred in other European countries, especially France.

The big question is how far people can keep their own traditions while also sharing the British values and culture that could bring us all closer together. Clearly when newcomers are asked to integrate into British society, it is important that they are welcomed and not discriminated against or treated unfairly. Building a more tolerant and cohesive society, based on mutual respect and a shared sense of being British, will be a challenging but vital task.

Key terms

Community cohesion People sharing a sense of belonging and community identity.

Sample exam questions: Citizenship, identity and community in the United Kingdom

Try these questions for the short-course exam (answers on page 99).

1. What is the best description of an asylum seeker?
   i. Someone applying for a British passport.
   ii. A person who is an illegal immigrant.
   iii. Someone on a waiting list for emigration.
   iv. A person wanting refuge and protection.   *(1 mark)*

2. State one reason why people in the UK often have a complex sense of identity.   (1 mark)

3. State one example of a British value.   (1 mark)

4. Explain why the United Kingdom is one of the most diverse societies in the world with a wide variety of ethnic groups and languages. In your answer, you should:
   - Give suitable examples of the ethnic groups that have settled in the UK.
   - Explain why at least two of these ethnic groups came to live in the UK.   *(4 marks)*

5. Evaluate the following viewpoint: 'Community cohesion is strong in all communities across the United Kingdom.' In your answer, you should:
   - Explain what community cohesion is and describe what a cohesive community might be like.
   - Describe any communities that lack community cohesion and explain why this might be the case.
   - Use evidence or examples to support the points you make.
   - Evaluate how far you agree that 'community cohesion is strong in all communities across the United Kingdom'.   *(12 marks)*

How do the police, CPS and criminal courts uphold the law and deal with people accused of crime?

Why do we have laws?

The law exists to control our behaviour. We might not agree with all the laws but everyone is expected to obey every law. We cannot choose only to obey the laws that we agree with. If we ignored laws that we didn't like, then there would be no common code of behaviour. People would never know what to expect from other members of their community and they would find it difficult to trust others.

Law and order would also break down if laws were applied unfairly to some groups but not to others. There would be protests and people might lose respect for the police. Laws work best when:

- Most people know about the law, and agree with it.
- The law is clear and easy to understand.
- The law is enforced easily and without discrimination.
- Punishments are clear and fair.

What are criminal offences?

There are many different types of crime but they can usually be placed in one of three categories.

1 Crimes against property such as theft or burglary.
2 Crimes against people's health and safety such as assault or robbery.
3 Crimes against the **Crown** such as perjury or treason.

The law also deals with disputes about such things as contracts, including marriage contracts and land ownership. These are matters of civil law rather than criminal law, as long as nobody has been hurt and no property has been damaged or stolen.

What is the role of the police?

The police have a legal responsibility to uphold the law and protect people from crime. They also have a legal responsibility to record crimes that are reported to them. They will go on to investigate most crime reports on behalf of the Crown (the Queen, the Government and citizens of the UK). The police have the legal right to stop, search and arrest someone in connection with a crime and charge them with an offence. The accused person is entitled to legal help and advice.

Who decides to take cases to court?

The decision about whether or not to take a case to court is made by the **Crown Prosecution Service** (CPS). The trained lawyers who work for the CPS have to decide whether the matter is serious enough to go to court and whether there is a good chance of the Crown winning the case.

Key terms

Crown The state or government. In the UK, the King or Queen is the head of the state or government. This is why the term 'Crown' is used.

Crown Prosecution Service (CPS) The CPS considers the information provided by the police about the activities of alleged criminals. The CPS decides whether there is enough evidence to take the matter to court and whether to do so would be in the public interest.

How are the courts organised?

Criminal cases start in the **Magistrates Court**. The less serious cases may be tried and sentenced there, especially if the accused person (defendant) pleads guilty. Magistrates are trained people who listen to the evidence and decide what to do with the defendant. Magistrates send more serious offences, such as robbery, to the **Crown Court** for trial. In the Crown Court, a **judge** and **jury** will listen to the evidence. The jury decides whether the defendant is guilty or not guilty. They must do this before being told about any other crimes carried out by the defendant in the past. The judge advises the jury on points of law, makes sure the trial is fair and decides the sentence. He or she takes the defendant's other offences (if any) into account. (People under the age of eighteen are usually tried in a **Youth Court**.)

In all English and Welsh criminal cases the Crown, on behalf of the people, prosecutes the defendant. It is not up to the crime victim or his legal representative to do this. The victim is likely to be called by the Crown to give evidence as a witness.

What happens to victims of crime?

If found guilty, a defendant may be fined. Any fine goes to the Crown. It is not paid to the victim. The victim may get some **compensation** and any stolen property returned to them. The police will return any property that they find. The victim is also likely to be offered support and advice from an independent charity called Victim Support. Victims of violent crime can apply to the Criminal Injuries Compensation Board. This is a government agency that pays compensation to victims. Compensation is not paid directly by the criminal.

How does crime threaten human rights?

What is it like to be a crime victim?

Crime can affect people in many different ways. People are surprised by how emotional they feel after being a victim of crime. These strong emotions can make crime victims feel unsettled and confused. Friends, partners and children of crime victims may also be upset.

The effects of crime can last for a long time. Serious crimes that cause physical harm, emotional stress or take away freedom can have serious effects on long-term health. Even if other people do not think of the crime as very serious, victims may still find they have a severe reaction. For example, a burglary can affect someone's life just as badly as an assault, even though nobody may have been physically hurt during the burglary.

Most victims of crime do not suffer any long-term harm. But some people do develop long-term problems, such as depression or anxiety-related illnesses. Others become afraid of going out and lose trust for

Key terms

Compensation A sum of money paid in return for any loss or damage someone has suffered.

Crown Court The court used by the state or government for trials of serious criminal offences.

Judge A legally trained and experienced lawyer who keeps order during a trial, advises the jury and decides sentences.

Jury A group of ordinary people aged eighteen and over. In a Crown Court the jury decides whether an accused person is guilty or not guilty.

Magistrates Court A court through which all criminal cases pass. Serious cases are sent to the Crown Court for trial. Some minor criminal matters are tried in the Magistrates Court, which also grants licences for the sale of alcohol and other potentially controversial local matters.

Youth Court A court where young people under eighteen are tried for criminal offences. Trials are conducted less formally than in an adult court and may not be reported in the media.

other people. Some people who have their house broken into feel unable to live there any more, as their personal space has been violated.

Crime also has an economic cost. The victim may have to replace many possessions. This takes time and is stressful. They may also need time off work, which could mean a loss of wages.

One of the things that can make crime hard to cope with is knowing that it was committed deliberately. Unlike an accident or illness, where there is normally no harm intended, people who commit a crime have done it with intention to cause harm. If you are the victim, this can make you feel very powerless and vulnerable.

Table C. Selected articles from the European Convention on Human Rights

Article 2	You have the right to life.
Article 3	No one has the right to hurt you or torture you.
Article 5	You have the right to liberty. If you are arrested, you have the right to know why. If you are arrested, you have the right to stand trial soon, or be released until the trial takes place.
Article 8	You have the right to respect for your private and family life, your home and correspondence.
Article 9	You have the right to freedom of thought, conscience and religion.
Article 10	You have the right to say and write what you think, as long as it does not harm others. You have the right to give and receive information from others.

? Study Table C. It contains some of the rights from the European Convention on Human Rights. Highlight those rights that might be threatened by crime.

How are human rights protected by the Universal Declaration of Human Rights, the Human Rights Act and international humanitarian law?

What are human rights?

The basis of all human rights is respect for each individual human life and for human dignity. Human rights do not have to be bought, earned or inherited. They belong to all of us simply because we are human. We all have a responsibility to safeguard human rights and not to take them away from anyone.

The Universal Declaration of Human Rights

After the Second World War ended in 1945, people felt it was important for the **United Nations** (UN) to draw up a Universal Declaration of Human Rights. This sets out the basic human rights and responsibilities everyone should enjoy. While these rights and rsponsibilities are not laws that each country must follow, they do help us to measure the human rights record of different governments across the world.

Key terms

United Nations (UN) An international organisation to which most countries of the world belong. It aims to promote peace, prevent war and maintain world security.

Article 1 of the Declaration states:

'All human beings are born free and equal in dignity and rights. They are endowed with reason and conscience and should act towards one another in a spirit of brotherhood.'

The other 29 articles from the Declaration include the following:

- Everyone has the right to a fair trial by an unbiased and independent judge. (Article 6)
- All are equal before the law. (Article 7)
- Everyone has the right to freedom of thought, conscience and religion. (Article 9)
- You have the right to take part in peaceful meetings and set up and join groups to protect or promote your interests. (Article 11)
- If you think that your rights have been denied to you, you can make an official complaint. (Article 13)
- Marriage shall be entered into only with the free and full consent of the intending spouses. (Article 16)
- Everyone has a right to education. (Article 26)

The European Court of Human Rights (ECtHR)

The **Council of Europe** built on the Universal Declaration of Human Rights to produce the European Convention on Human Rights (ECHR) in 1950. European citizens can appeal to the **European Court of Human Rights** (ECtHR) if they feel the laws in their own country have not protected their rights.

The ECtHR gives European citizens the following legal rights:

- Life, liberty and security of the person.
- A fair trial in civil and criminal matters.
- The right for citizens of voting age to vote and be a candidate in elections.
- Freedom of thought, conscience and religion.
- Freedom of expression.
- Property or peaceful enjoyment of possessions.
- Freedom of assembly and association.

The following are prohibited:

- Torture and inhuman or degrading treatment or punishment.
- The death penalty.
- Slavery and forced labour.
- Discrimination in the enjoyment of rights included in the European Convention on Human Rights.

Below are some examples of cases brought to the ECtHR (the Court):

- Unlawful killings.
- Torture and ill treatment of prisoners.
- Telephone tapping.
- Discrimination against homosexuals.

The Human Rights Act 1988

By passing the Human Rights Act, the UK Government brought nearly all the rights from the European Convention on Human Rights into UK law. All public bodies such as the police, schools, hospitals and armed forces must make sure they respect the rights contained in the Human Rights Act. If they do not, they can be taken to court.

Key terms

Council of Europe An organisation of more than 40 European states, founded in 1949, which protects human rights through international agreement. It should not be confused with the European Council, which is a policy-making body of the EU.

European Court of Human Rights (ECtHR) A court that decides on cases in which it is claimed there has been a breach of the European Convention on Human Rights.

International humanitarian law

International humanitarian law is a set of rules that aims to protect people's rights in times of war. It protects people who are not or are no longer fighting. It also places limits on the weapons and tactics that can be used in war.

The seven basic international rules of conflict

1 People not taking part in the fighting should have their lives and integrity protected by all sides in the conflict.

2 An enemy who surrenders should not be killed or injured.

3 Wounded and sick people should be collected and cared for by whichever side comes across them. The emblem of the red cross or the red crescent is the sign of such protection and must be respected.

4 All captured fighters and civilians are entitled to respect for their lives, dignity, personal rights and convictions. They shall have the right to contact their families and to receive aid.

5 Everyone shall be entitled to a fair trial if they are accused of doing something wrong. No-one shall be physically or mentally tortured, or given physical punishment or suffer cruel or degrading treatment.

6 Weapons or methods of warfare that cause unnecessary losses or excessive suffering should not be used.

7 Fighters should always respect civilians and their property. Civilians should not be attacked. All attacks should be against other fighters or military targets.

Key terms

International humanitarian law A set of rules that aims to protect people's rights in wartime. It protects people who are not or are no longer fighting. It also places limits on the weapons and tactics that can be used in war.

⬆ **Women in Eritrea read a leaflet about their rights under international humanitarian law.**

? Interpreting international humanitarian law

Use the information from the seven rules of international conflict above to decide which of the following actions would be illegal under international humanitarian law.

- Bombing a factory making weapons.
- Firing a nuclear missile at an enemy city.
- Laying land mines outside a village.
- Leaving wounded soldiers for their own side to look after.

Case study – Anti-terrorism, Crime and Security Act 2001

On 11 September 2001, the United States of America was attacked by terrorists. People in the UK were worried that there would also be attacks in this country. The governments of the USA and the UK declared 'war on terrorism'. By the end of 2001, war in Afghanistan had led to a major defeat for the Taliban (a political group that had supported attacks on the USA). The governments of the USA and Britain also made legal changes to prevent further terrorism. By Christmas 2001, the British Parliament had passed the Anti-terrorism, Crime and Security **Act** as an emergency measure. A similar act was still in force in 2009.

Nearly everyone agreed that the terror attacks on the USA were wrong, but there was some disagreement over the actions of the UK Government. Some people were worried that a clampdown on terrorism would limit the human rights of ordinary people in Britain. Others felt that because the Government supported the war in Afghanistan, it was also guilty of terrorism by a state against innocent people.

These disagreements led to heated debates on TV, in the newspapers and in Parliament itself. Political parties, pressure groups and religious organisations all joined in. While getting the Anti-terrorism **Bill** through Parliament, the Government suffered defeats in the House of Lords and had to make some changes to its plans. Almost as soon as the Act was passed, suspected terrorists were arrested.

The terrorist attacks on the USA on 11 September 2001 led to restrictions on everyone's freedom.

How do rights compete and conflict?

Rights can sometimes compete and conflict with one another.

Security vs privacy

For example, under Article 8 of the ECHR, people have the right to respect for their correspondence (letters, emails, phone conversations). In 2009 the UK Government arranged for all emails and records of phone conversations to be available to the police. The Government decided that access to such information would help the police track down criminals and improve our security. So, in this case, the Government felt that people's right to life and security was more important than their right to privacy.

Freedom of expression vs encouraging hatred

Another area of frequent conflict involves Article 10 of the ECHR, freedom of expression. The ECHR makes it clear that that you have to say and write what you think in a responsible way. However, this leaves quite a lot to a person's own judgement. He or she may speak out in a way that encourages hatred of a particular religious or cultural group. This would then be a criminal offence as the rights of people belonging to those groups would be under threat.

Press freedom vs privacy

There are often conflicts about whether the **media** have a right to write stories that may cause embarrassment to individuals and their families. The press are allowed to do this if the story is true and if they can show that the news is 'in the public interest'.

Case Study – Max Mosley's battle for privacy

In 2009 the *News of the World* published details of Max Mosley's private life that were only partly true and were also embarrassing and damaging to him and his family. Max Mosley took his case to the High Court and won £60,000 in damages from the newspaper.

Following his victory in the **High Court**, Max Mosley wanted to force the UK Government to introduce a new privacy law that would set out journalists' responsibilities more clearly. He asked the European Court of Human Rights to force journalists to approach people in any news story before publication to let them know of any allegations against them. The person who is the subject of the story would then be able to ask a judge to stop the publication if it was an infringement of their privacy.

Key terms

High Court The court that deals with the most important and high value cases in England and Wales.

How does the law help when rights compete or conflict, or where people want to protect or promote their rights?

Using the courts to put things right

In a case where you think that your privacy has been has been invaded by the press, you can use the courts to prevent publication of the article or, if that is too late, you can claim **damages** from the media company that is responsible.

As no criminal offence has been committed, you will need to use civil law to achieve this. As the police and CPS can only help if a crime has been committed, you have to take the case to court yourself or get a lawyer to help you. This is a complex and expensive business. There is a risk that you may get no damages and will end up paying thousands of pounds to cover the legal fees of both sides. The case may also receive even more attention than the press coverage to which you are objecting. Some people are now using the Human Rights Act to help protect their private and family lives.

The Data Protection Act

Schools, hospitals, businesses, the revenue service and a range of other organisations collect personal information about us. They do this so that our details can be recalled quickly and easily when we make contact with an enquiry.

However, this storage of data is also a threat to our privacy and could lead to identity theft. The Data Protection Act allows the storage of data as long as certain strict rules are followed. These rules include asking for your consent before certain types of sensitive data about you are stored.

You can use the Data Protection Act to check the data held about you and to get it put right if it is incorrect.

What responsibilities do citizens have to obey the law and support the justice system?

Should people always obey the law?

All citizens have a responsibility to find out about the laws that apply to them and to obey those laws. Breaking a law because you did not know about it is not accepted as an excuse.

Some people object to certain laws and break them to draw attention to the problem. One of the most famous examples of this is when suffragettes committed crimes of damage and violence in the early part of the twentieth century to draw attention to the problem of women not having the right to vote. However, there is no evidence that this law-breaking persuaded the Government to give in to their demands.

The Freedom of Information Act

The Freedom of Information Act (2000) is a law that gives everyone the right to ask for information held by any public body in England, Wales or Northern Ireland. (Public bodies include schools, hospitals, local authorities, the police and departments of national government.) Requests must get a response within twenty working days. Public bodies can refuse to release private information about other people or information that might damage the security of other people or property.

The Freedom of Information Act enables people get information that may help them to protect or promote their rights.

Key terms

Damages Money awarded by a court to compensate someone for the loss or injury they have suffered.

Media Newspapers, TV, the internet and any other means of communicating ideas or information.

If we all decided to obey only those laws that we agreed with, people's behaviour would become less predictable and our society would be a more dangerous and much less orderly place.

What responsibilities do citizens have to support the justice system?

Making a citizens' arrest

Anyone can arrest another person if that person has committed a criminal offence, or if they are about to assault someone. You can also arrest someone who has escaped from prison. Citizens are allowed to use reasonable force to do this, but they often get into trouble with the police themselves if the arrested person claims that they have been hurt or kidnapped. This is especially likely to happen if the person arrested is a teenager and the person carrying out the arrest is an adult. For this reason, the police do not encourage ordinary people to carry out arrests.

Assisting the police

The police are employed to uphold the law and protect the peace. They do this on behalf of the public and police wages are paid out of the taxes we all pay. As the police are working on our behalf, most people are happy to help them where necessary. Some people become special constables or police cadets to provide practical help on a day-to-day basis. It is a criminal offence to deliberately obstruct the police in carrying out their duty.

Being a witness in court

The justice system relies on witnesses to give statements to the police and appear in court. Without witness statements, trials would collapse and offenders would go unpunished. Sometimes people are reluctant to become official witnesses, as giving a statement can take time and be a stressful experience. Some people are also afraid that the defendant will attempt to threaten witnesses. To make things easier for witnesses, the Witness Service assists witnesses and shows them what might be expected in court.

Jury service

Each year, many ordinary people are chosen for jury service. A jury consists of twelve members of the public selected at random. Jurors usually try the more serious criminal cases such as murder, rape, assault, burglary or fraud. These trials take place in the Crown Court.

Receiving a jury summons means you are legally required to attend court. Jury service is one of the most important civic duties that anyone can be asked to perform. As a juror, you have a chance to play a vital part in the legal system. You do not need any knowledge of the legal system. Each individual juror will be asked to consider the evidence presented and then decide whether the defendant is guilty or not guilty.

© Metropolitan Police Authority, 2009

One way to assist the police is to become a volunteer police officer. This Metropolitan Police advert makes the point that anyone over the age of eighteen can volunteer in this way.

What are the rights and responsibilities of citizens and the police?

Rights and responsibilities of the citizen

Rights
- To be treated fairly, according to the law and without any discrimination.
- To be given an explanation before any search is carried out.
- To be given the name and contact details of the officer carrying out a search.
- To be searched in private by an officer of the same sex if the search involves more than removing outer clothing such as a coat or jacket.
- To refuse permission for police to search your house or flat unless they have a search warrant.
- To be given a reason for an arrest.
- When arrested, not to be interviewed until you are taken to a police station.
- Not to be interviewed formally before being advised about your rights and cautioned.
- To inform someone of your arrest.
- To receive legal advice when arrested.
- If under seventeen or with learning difficulties, to have an 'appropriate adult', usually a parent, present at the interview.
- To be able to read the police codes of practice and be told your rights.
- To remain silent or to refuse to answer questions.
- Not normally to be detained for more than 24 hours without being charged.
- To receive an official custody record when you are released.

Responsibilities
- To obey the law.
- Not to obstruct the police.
- Not to attempt to destroy evidence.
- To co-operate with your legal adviser.

Rights and responsibilities of the police

Rights
- To expect co-operation from citizens.
- To stop anyone in a public place and ask them to account for their actions.
- To stop and search people who they reasonably suspect may have committed or be about to commit a crime.
- To arrest someone if they are committing a criminal offence, have committed an offence or are about to do so.
- To use reasonable force to stop, search or arrest people.
- To enter premises without permission to save life, or to deal with or prevent a crime.
- To seize someone's property if they think it may have been stolen or if it is evidence linked to a crime.
- To detain someone for up to 24 hours without charge.
- To charge someone if they feel they have enough evidence.

Responsibilities
- To uphold the law, protect human life and keep the peace.
- To record any offence brought to their attention.
- To be polite and treat people with respect.
- To give people their name and contact details.
- To obey the law themselves.
- To follow all the codes of practice for dealing with citizens.
- To make accurate statements to a court of law.
- To only use reasonable force as a last resort.
- To avoid any form of discrimination.

How does a Bill pass through the UK Parliament to become an Act and new law?

The party manifesto

The **political party** with the most MPs will usually form the Government. People voted for the party because they liked what was promised in their election manifesto. The Government needs to keep its promises by making new laws.

Government policy

The Government reviews its election manifesto and decides what is urgent and needs doing first. These ideas are put into the Queen's Speech at the official opening of a new Parliament. The Queen's Speech sets out the Government's priorities.

Green Papers and White Papers

The Government consults experts and the public on what should be included in the new law. A Green Paper invites comments on the main ideas for change. This is followed by a White Paper that consults people on the likely detail of the new law.

The report stage and Third Reading

The committee take the Bill back to Parliament to report on any changes that have been made.

The Third Reading of the Bill is where MPs vote on the final version. If MPs vote in favour, the Bill goes on to its next stage.

The committee stage

A smaller group of MPs or members of the **House of Lords** now looks at the Bill in more detail to see whether the proposed change in the law will be fair and will work. MPs may suggest changes called amendments to improve the new law.

The first parliamentary reading

The Government uses the comments from consultation on the White Paper to draw up a Bill or proposal for the new law. MPs in the **House of Commons** debate the general principles of the Bill. If MPs vote in favour, the Bill goes to its next stage.

The House of Lords

The Bill then goes to the House of Lords, where peers debate it and may suggest further changes for MPs to consider in the House of Commons.

The democratically elected MPs in the House of Commons can ignore the changes suggested by the Lords.

The Royal Assent

The Queen, as Head of State, has to give her final approval to the Bill before it becomes an Act of Parliament and a new law. This is a formality. The Queen believes it to be her duty to approve the Bills of her democratically elected government.

Key terms

House of Commons The 646 democratically elected MPs form the House of Commons.

House of Lords Members of the House of Lords (peers) either inherit their position or are chosen for their wisdom by the leaders of the main political parties. Peers debate new laws and offer their advice on possible changes.

Political party A group of people with similar views who form an organisation to get its members elected to government (either local or national).

Where can people get legal advice and support?

There are four main sources of legal advice and support.

A solicitor

Solicitors are legally trained and usually work as part of a team in which each partner specialises in one or two branches of the law. Legal partnerships or firms of solicitors are businesses that aim to make a profit from their services. Legal advice and support is expensive, but many solicitors offer the first half hour of advice for free, so that people can decide whether it is worth going further.

People with low incomes are entitled to Legal Aid. This means that they can obtain legal advice and support free of charge should they need it.

Some solicitors will offer to work on a 'no win, no fee' basis. This applies to cases where they offer to help people claim damages if they have been injured as a result of someone else's mistakes. The solicitor's fees are taken out of any damages awarded – often leaving very little for the victim.

A trade union, employers' association or membership organisation

Trade unions will provide legal support and advice to members who have problems at work, such as contractual disputes, bullying or unfair dismissal. Employers' associations such as the Confederation of British Industry and the Institute of Directors provide legal advice and support to business over issues to do with contacts and trade disputes. People who join associations such as the Automobile Association (AA), Royal Automobile CLlub (RAC) or the Cyclists' Touring Club (CTC) can benefit from the association or club's legal advice and support in cases of accident, damage or other problems connected with their car or bicycle.

Rights and advice websites run by charities or the government

There are several good websites run by charities. Some of the best in 2009 were:

- Adviceguide. Offers online advice from the charity Citizens Advice. *www.adviceguide.org.uk*
- TheSite.org. This website is owned and run by YouthNet UK, a registered charity founded in 1995. *www.thesite.org*
- Which? The Consumers' Association is a charity that tests and gives impartial advice on a wide range of consumer products as well as offering legal advice on the purchase of goods and services. *www.which.co.uk*

These sites concentrate on telling people what their rights are and advising what they should do to enforce them. These websites often advise on how to deal with a problem without having to use a solicitor, except as a last resort. They can be a very good source of initial advice.

Finally, the Government has its their own website to inform citizens about their rights. This is a very useful site that includes information ranging from which school to choose for a child to what to do about problems with the neighbours. *www.direct.gov.uk*

The Citizens Advice Bureau

Citizens Advice Bureaus are based in most large towns and cities. They are run by the independent charity Citizens Advice and are staffed largely by trained volunteers. People can see an adviser without an appointment and the adviser will direct them to the correct organisation or public body to help with their problem.

Sample exam questions: Fairness and justice in decision-making and the law

Try these questions for the short-course exam (answers on pages 99–100).

6. What is the best description of a Crown Court?
   i. A court where disputes about contracts and property ownership are decided.
   ii. A court which settles disputes that occur in Parliament.
   iii. A court that deals with serious criminal cases.
   iv. An appeal court where people go if they are not satisfied with the judgement of a lower court. *(1 mark)*

7. State one example of a criminal offence. *(1 mark)*

8. State one basic rule that governments should follow under international humanitarian law. *(1 mark)*

9. Explain why criminal behaviour may threaten human rights. In your answer, you should:
   - Give suitable examples of criminal behaviour to support your answer.
   - Explain which human rights are likely to be under threat as a result of criminal behaviour. *(4 marks)*

10. Evaluate the following viewpoint: 'The right to privacy must be protected at all costs. There is no more important right than this.' In your answer, you should:
   - Explain why the right to privacy is important and describe how it is protected.
   - Use evidence or examples to support the points you make.
   - Describe other rights that may be equally important or more important than the right to privacy.
   - Evaluate how far you agree that 'there is no more important right' than the right to privacy.
   (12 marks)

? Which sources of legal advice and support do you suggest would be best in the example cases below?

Example cases
- A couple want to separate, but there are problems about how to divide the property.
- A family has been evicted from their flat and has nowhere to go.
- A worker has had his contract altered by his or her employer without any consultation.
- A mobile phone is faulty but the shop it was bought from refuses to help.
- Someone is unsure what to do if they were ever arrested by the police.

2.3 Democracy and voting

How are decisions made at school and in the wider community?

At school

- Students make decisions in tutor groups, year groups or houses.
- Students vote for Student Council representatives.
- The Student Council decides on issues in school.
- Parents vote for School Governors.
- School Governors decide about what should happen in the school.

In the community

- Citizens make decisions in neighbourhood groups, community associations and residents' associations.
- Citizens vote for parish, town, borough, district, city or regional councillors.
- Citizens vote in local referendums (votes on a particular issue) when these are held.
- Councils or Local Authorities decide on issues in the community.

Complete the grid below to show examples of decisions made in your school and community.

School or community body	Example of a decision with an impact on school or community life
The Student Council	
The School Governors	
Your Local Authority or Council	

How has the right to vote been extended in the United Kingdom (UK)?

Table D. History of the right to vote

1832	Act of Parliament gives voting rights to the richest 15 per cent of men.
1838–48	A pressure group (The Chartists) campaigns for voting rights for all.
1859	Liberal Party formed. It promises to extend voting rights.
1871	Workers gain the right to form trade unions.
1884	Vote extended to the wealthiest 60 per cent of men over 21.
1897–1918	Women campaign for the right to vote.
1906	Labour Party founded. It campaigns for all adults to have the vote.

Table D continued

1914–18	First World War. Women prove they can do 'mens' jobs'.
1918	All men over 21 gain the right to vote. So do women over 30.
1928	Women gain the right to vote at 21.
1969	Voting age cut from 21 to 18.
2009	Should the voting age be cut to 16? Should prisoners have the right to vote?

⬇ **Women were prepared to break the law to gain the right to vote.**

Womens' campaign for the right to vote

The move for women to have the vote started in 1897, when Millicent Fawcett founded the National Union of Women's Suffrage. Progress was slow and, in 1903, Emmeline Pankhurst and her daughters Christabel and Sylvia founded the Women's Social and Political Union (WSPU). They wanted women to have the right to vote, and they were not prepared to wait. The WSPU became better known as the Suffragettes. Members of the Suffragettes were prepared to use violence to get what they wanted.

However, when the First World War started in 1914, the Pankhursts stopped the campaign of violence and supported the Government in the effort to win the war. The work done by women in the war was vital, and in 1918 women over 30 were given the right to vote.

How are power and authority different in democratic and non-democratic societies?

Power and authority in a democracy

In a **democracy**, **power** is in the hands of all the citizens. Each citizen has the right to vote, form a **political party**, join a pressure group and campaign for what they believe in.

In a democracy, **authority** (the right to make and implement decisions on behalf of others) is held by elected politicians. Civil servants (government administrators) have authority because they carry out the decisions made by the politicians. Judges have authority because they interpret and uphold the law. In a democracy, judges are independent of the elected politicians. This means that although politicians make the law in the first place, they cannot interfere with the decisions made by judges.

Examples of countries with democratically elected governments include the United Kingdom, Germany, India, Thailand, Australia, South Africa, Brazil, the United States of America and Russia. Most of the world's nations are democracies.

Key terms

Authority Having the right to use power.

Democracy A system of government in which decisions are taken either by the population directly, or through representatives they have elected.

General election An election to choose the MPs who will form a new parliament. A general election is held at least once every five years.

Media Newspapers, TV, the internet and any other means of communicating ideas or information.

Power Making decisions that affect others.

Power and authority in non-democratic systems of government

Dictatorships and single-party states are both examples of non-democratic forms of government.

In a dictatorship or single-party state, power is in the hands of one person, a small group of people or the leaders of a single political party. There are no **general elections** and no rival political parties.

People who become members of the single political party have the right to discuss its policies and to choose its leaders.

Any campaigns against the government are stamped out. Authority is held by the leading group, or single political party, and by the civil service, the police and the judges they control.

Examples of countries with non-democratic governments include Saudi Arabia, China, North Korea, the United Arab Emirates and Myanmar (Burma).

A poster from the 1960s shows smiling Chinese workers reading the *Thoughts* (sayings) of Mao Zedong (the first Chinese Communist leader). In reality, many people were unhappy living in a country where human rights were limited.

Why are human rights likely to be under threat in non-democratic societies?

In a democracy people have the right to use their vote to get rid of an unpopular government. There are regular elections. (In the UK elections are held at least every five years and, in the United States, citizens elect their president every four years.) If citizens are generally unhappy with their government, they are usually prepared to wait for the next election and vote for a different set of politicians. If citizens feel strongly about something, they can campaign for change between elections. Citizens can also campaign to persuade political parties to adopt new ideas.

In a democracy, the media is free to support the government or to support a rival political party. Peaceful protests or demonstrations are allowed, even if they are against the government. Most democracies are relatively peaceful and stable because citizens know that they can express their views freely and that change is possible.

People who live in a country with a non-democratic government have no right to vote for a different government. To stay popular, the non-democratic government tries to control the media so that only good news about the government and its leaders is printed and broadcast. People are encouraged to support the government by, for example, joining the single political party. By joining, people find it easier to get a well-paid job and they can have some influence on decision-making.

Non-democratic governments use the police and the army to discourage protest. Opponents of the government are likely to be imprisoned or expelled from the country. Their families may also be discriminated against or subjected to violence.

A Japanese reporter filming anti-government protests in Myanmar (Burma), 2007. He was shot and killed by soldiers as they fired to disperse the crowd.

Why are human rights likely to be protected in democratic societies?

Study the grid below. Link the human rights in Table E overleaf with the human rights listed in the grid by filling in the empty column.

Features of a democracy	Articles of the European Convention on Human Rights linked to this feature
All citizens have the right to vote.	
Citizens are free to vote for whoever they choose.	
Citizens vote in secret.	
All citizens have freedom of speech.	
Citizens can form their own political parties.	
Citizens are free to join or form pressure groups.	
Citizens have a right to complain or protest.	
The media is free to express opinions.	
All citizens have the same legal rights.	
Citizens have the right to a fair trial within a reasonable time.	
Judges are independent from the government.	
The law protects citizens from wrongful treatment by the government.	

Table E. Selected articles from the European Convention on Human Rights

Article 5	You have the right to liberty. If you are arrested, you have the right to know why. If you are arrested, you have the right to stand trial soon, or be released until the trial takes place.
Article 6	You have the right to a fair trial by an unbiased and independent judge. You have the right to be assisted by a lawyer who has to be paid by the government if you are poor.
Article 9	You have the right to freedom of thought, conscience and religion.
Article 10	You have the right to say and write what you think, as long as it does not harm others. You have the right to give and receive information from others.
Article 11	You have the right to take part in peaceful meetings and set up and join groups to protect or promote your interests.
Article 13	If you think that your rights have been denied, you can make an official complaint.
Article 14	You have your rights whatever your skin colour, sex, language, political or religious beliefs or origins.
Article 3 of Protocol 1	You have the right to elect the government of your country through a secret vote.

What is a representative democracy?

Democracy means the rule of the people. Each individual in a democracy has a vote about what to do. There is no queen, king or supreme ruler, and anybody can suggest a new law.

The earliest democracy in the world began in Athens, now the capital city of Greece, in 510BC. Athens was one of several Greek states. When democracy proved to be successful in Athens, many other Greek states chose it for their government, too. Only adult male citizens who owned land or their own houses had the right to vote. Men would go to a meeting place to vote on the issues of the day while their slaves did most of the work. This system of government, with frequent and direct voting by citizens, is known as **classical democracy.**

A problem for classical democracies was that it was very inconvenient for men to always be going to the meeting-place to vote. Even Greek citizens had some work to do and they couldn't always be voting. So most classical democracies sooner or later ended up choosing a few men who would do most of the voting and do their best to represent the other citizens. The others only came when there was a really important vote. This system has become known as **representative democracy.**

Key terms

Classical democracy A form of democracy in which citizens vote frequently and directly on issues of the day.

Representative democracy A form of democracy in which citizens choose representatives, who vote on issues and do their best to represent all citizens.

It was hard to decide how to choose these few men, and different states did it different ways. Athens did it by a lottery. If you got the winning ticket then you were on the Council of 500. Men served for a year.

Representative democracies now choose those men and women who will represent the rest by holding elections. Anyone can stand for election as a **candidate** and they campaign to get as many votes from the other citizens as possible. At first, most of the representatives were popular or important people in their communities. As populations grew and communications improved, people standing for election would get together with other candidates with similar views to form a political party. This makes it easier for voters to decide who to vote for. They may not know the candidates standing for election in their **constituency** but they can find out which political party they prefer and vote for the candidate representing that party.

What is the difference between Parliament and the Government? How does Parliament make the government accountable to the citizens?

The UK Parliament is not the same as the Government. In fact it is the job of Parliament to check on the actions of the Government and to make sure that citizens' interests are being safeguarded.

What does Parliament do?

- Members of Parliament debate the major issues of the day.
- Parliament receives reports from the **Prime Minister** and other members of the Government.
- Once each week, any Member of Parliament (MP) can ask questions, and the Prime Minister must attend Parliament to answer them.
- MPs examine and discuss Government proposals for new laws.
- MPs vote on new laws.
- MPs vote on the Government's plans for raising and spending money.

In these ways, Parliament makes sure that Government actions are always examined and questioned.

What is the connection between Parliament and the Government?

After an election, the 646 newly elected MPs form a new Parliament. The political party with the most MPs forms the Government.

The Queen invites the leader of the largest political party to become Prime Minister. The Prime Minister then chooses some of the most experienced and skilled MPs in his or her political party to help run the country. These senior MPs meet with the Prime Minister at least once a week to discuss the major issues facing the country. This group of senior MPs is known as the **Cabinet**.

Key terms

Cabinet The Prime Minister and the senior MPs he or she has chosen to help run the country. There are usually around twenty people in the Cabinet.

Candidate A person who asks people to vote for him or her as their representative.

Constituency An area of the country with around 60,000 voters. Each of the 646 constituencies in the UK elects one MP to Parliament.

Prime Minister The Prime Minister is leader of one of the political parties in Parliament – usually the party with the most MPs. He or she is asked by the Queen to select the Government to run the country.

What does the Government do?

- The Government proposes new laws to Parliament.
- It draws up plans for raising and spending money.
- It makes sure that new laws are put into action by instructing **civil servants** to carry out Government **policy**.
- It responds to emergencies and deals with day-to-day issues. For example, the Government will send emergency aid to another country without asking for Parliament's permission first.

How can citizens play an active part in local and national elections?

Everyone aged eighteen and over, except convicted prisoners and members of the House of Lords, can vote in UK elections. A general election to choose MPs for the UK Parliament takes place at least once every five years.

To be able to vote, you need to be on the **Register of Electors**. This is easy. Each year a registration form is sent to every house or flat in the country. You simply put your name on the form and send it back. Then you will get an invitation to vote every time there is an election.

You may be asked to vote by post or by going to a special place called a polling station. This is usually a local library, school or church hall. Voting is secret. You just mark a cross next to the name of the person you want to vote for.

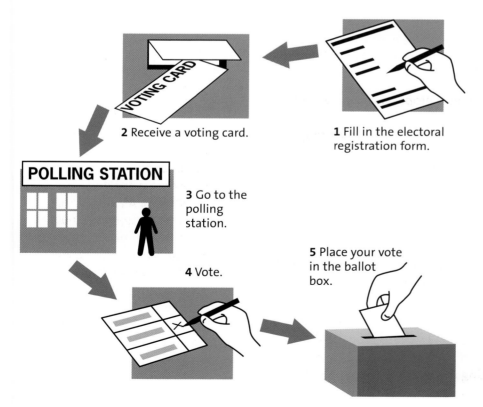

2 Receive a voting card.

1 Fill in the electoral registration form.

POLLING STATION

3 Go to the polling station.

5 Place your vote in the ballot box.

4 Vote.

How to cast your vote.

Voting in elections is an important way of joining in the democratic process. We can choose the representative whose views most closely match our own.

To get more fully involved, people over eighteen can be candidates in an election. If they get enough votes, they will attend meetings to represent the people who voted for them.

Most election candidates have already joined a political party. When you join a political party, you meet with other party members to come up with ideas for improving your local area or the country as a whole. There are several political parties in the UK and most people can find one that matches their own views.

How can citizens influence decision-making by joining political parties?

Anyone can join a political party or even start their own political party.

A political party is a group of people with similar ideas and viewpoints who organise themselves to fight elections. By gaining power in local and/or national elections, the political party can make changes to fit in with its ideas and viewpoints.

Table F. The three biggest political parties in the UK Parliament in 2009

Party	Membership fee	No. of MPs, 2009	Example of party's ideas or viewpoint
Conservative	£25	193	Give people more choice and control over the type of school and health service they use. Cut taxes but expect people to pay something towards the services they use.
Labour	£38	350	Use taxes from wealthier people to support poorer people and to improve services in health and education through government support and regulation.
Liberal Democrat	£10	63	Cut taxes to low- and middle-income earners, but also improve health and education services by making them more efficient under local control.

There are many other political parties in the UK, including the Scottish National Party (SNP), Plaid Cymru (the Welsh nationalists), the UK Independence Party (UKIP) and the Green Party.

People who join political parties can have a say in deciding the party's ideas and viewpoints. They contribute to the party's policies and can help to shape the **manifesto** given to voters before an election.

Members of political parties can:
- attend meetings of the party to decide on policies and campaigns
- help raise money to support the party
- give out leaflets and other publicity to voters
- campaign on local or national issues
- help to choose candidates for elections
- represent the party as a candidate in an election.

How can citizens influence decision-making by joining pressure groups?

Anyone can join a **pressure group**, or even start a pressure group of their own.

A pressure group is a group of people with similar views on a single issue. For example, the members of Greenpeace all want to protect the environment. A pressure group is different from a political party because it does not aim to form a government. Instead, a pressure group seeks to influence decision-making by persuading politicians and civil servants to take action on a particular issue.

Document 1

Extract adapted from the Amnesty International website (www.amnesty.org.uk) February 2009

 amnesty.co.uk

Amnesty is calling for the UK Government to take a lead in investigating abuses of international human rights in Gaza. These include Israeli attacks that have been directed at civilians or civilian buildings in the Gaza Strip and Palestinian rocket attacks directed at Israeli towns.

YOUR MESSAGE

Human rights in Gaza

I urge the UK Government to use all its diplomatic tools to push for an independent, international investigation that could help bring people to justice for crimes committed in the conflict.

Document 2

Extract adapted from the RSPCA Annual Review 2007

In June the European Commission adopted new guidelines for the housing and care of animals used in laboratories. Our scientific staff work alongside civil servants to help develop these guidelines. We are now meeting with politicians to persuade them that these improvements should be made compulsory and part of European law.

Key terms

Manifesto A document produced by a political party before an election, which sets out for voters what the party promises to do if it gets into power.

Pressure group A group of people with similar views on a single issue, who lobby elected representatives.

On its website, Amnesty International encourages supporters to pass on their views to the Government. After weeks of campaigning this particular Amnesty action was successful. The UK Government changed its position and now publicly supports the Goldstone Inquiry (a UN team investigationg possible war crimes in Gaza).

? Think of at least three ways in which pressure groups try to influence politicians. Documents 1 and 2 (left) and the photo overleaf may help you.

Students from Tamworth schools take part in the Hands Off Tamworth Schools Campaign, protesting against plans to turn their school into an academy and the loss of community sixth forms.

How does the media influence decision-making?

UK citizens get a lot of their information from newspapers, TV and the internet. This helps citizens to know what is going on. Keeping up to date with the news also helps citizens form opinions on issues such as whether it is right for the British army to be fighting in Afghanistan or whether university tuition fees should be increased.

The UK is unusual because the media organisation with the biggest influence, the **BBC**, is regulated and funded by the UK Government from money paid by the public through an annual **licence fee**. As a result, the BBC has to be impartial. This means that its reporters or programmes should not promote a particular viewpoint or support a particular political party. An advantage of this lack of bias is that people tend to trust the BBC for news. The BBC also produces the World Service, a radio station that broadcasts news across the world in 31 different languages. This helps to promote Britain and its culture around the world.

Key terms

BBC (British Broadcasting Corporation) The UK's publicly owned broadcasting company. It is regulated by a Royal Charter. This sets out its responsibilities to be impartial and also to inform, educate and entertain the public.

Licence fee The BBC is paid for directly through a fee paid by each household for any electronic device used for receiving TV programmes. This allows the BBC to run a wide range of popular public services for everyone without adverts and independent from the influence of advertisers, shareholders or politicians.

> **Extract from the BBC Royal Charter**
>
> The public purposes of the BBC are:
>
> - sustaining citizenship and civil society
> - promoting education and learning
> - stimulating creativity and cultural excellence
> - representing the UK, its nations, regions and communities
> - bringing the UK to the world and the world to the UK.

Other news organisations are owned privately. For example, *The Sun* and *The Times* newspapers are largely owned by the Murdoch family (Australian millionaires). The Murdochs also part-own Fox News (an American cable news channel). The Murdoch family like to have some control over the viewpoints expressed by the media they own. For example, in the 1997 UK general election, *The Sun* supported the Labour Party, using its front page to ask its 3 million readers to vote Labour. The decision to do this was made by Rupert Murdoch.

Privately owned media also run campaigns to pressurise the Government to take action. In 2009 the *Daily Telegraph* newspaper (owned by the Barclay brothers, who made their fortunes in property and **retailing**) ran a campaign called 'Justice for Pensioners'. This campaign aimed to persuade the Government to cut taxes for retired people. The campaign was supported by the Conservative Party and by the pressure group Age Concern. The same year, the *Daily Mirror* ran a campaign to persuade the Government to give more help to victims of diseases caused by asbestos. The newspaper called on the Government to spend more money on inspecting buildings containing asbestos and to make sure that it was removed safely.

How can citizens and politicians use the media?

Citizens often get information from the media when carrying out research on an issue or planning a campaign. For example, the BBC website is a favourite for Citizenship students as it shows both sides of an argument and has links to other relevant sources of information.

Many newspapers and websites have a 'letters page' or section where citizens can express their own views. Below is an example from the Radio 1 Newsbeat website.

Have Your Say
Adapted from BBC Radio 1 Newsbeat
news.bbc.co.uk/newsbeat/hi/have_your_say

What do you think of the G20 protests? Will they influence the G20 summit? Has your day been disrupted by the demonstrations?

Added: Friday 3 April 2009 10:08 GMT 11:08 UK

'I am glad that people feel strongly enough about something to protest about it, and glad that we live in a country that allows people to show their views.'

'I have just finished reading a book about the Soviet Union, it makes me so grateful that we live in Britain where we can fully show our views without any fear of punishment for having said the wrong thing.'

Citizens can set up and use personal **blogs** and websites to persuade others. A couple of people can form a small pressure group and, with a slick website, they can have considerable influence in spite of their small numbers.

Citizens running a campaign can use newspapers, radio and TV to gain publicity and encourage support from other people. Most pressure groups have a media or press officer. Their job is to write and send **press releases** to newspapers and to radio and TV stations. This has to be done frequently to keep the pressure group in the news, and to give an impression that the group's ideas are important and should be taken seriously by politicians.

Key terms

Blog A type of website, usually maintained by one person with regular entries of commentary, descriptions of events or other material such as graphics or video.

Press release Businesses, celebrities, politicians, pressure groups and charities write their own accounts of events or set out their opinions on an issue. They send this to newspapers, broadcasters and websites for publication.

Retailing Buying and selling. A retail business is a shop or other outlet for selling goods (for example an online bookseller).

The media has considerable influence on what citizens feel about politicians and their policies. As a result, politicians are keen to have good relations with reporters and media owners. Politicians are also keen to have a positive image in the media and sometimes hire media consultants to help them achieve this. Media consultants can help politicians adjust their hairstyles, style of dress or even the way they speak.

Why is a free press is important in a democracy?

In a democracy citizens have the chance to use their vote to decide which political party should form a government. Sometimes citizens have the chance to vote on a single issue in a **referendum**. For example, in 2008 the citizens of Manchester voted on whether motorists travelling into the city centre should pay a special tax called a congestion charge. The supporters of the charge hoped that it would reduce traffic and pollution, and encourage people to use buses, trains and trams. Fifty-three per cent of citizens voted in the referendum and eight out of ten people voted against bringing in the charge. The charge was not brought in.

Citizens have a responsibility to think carefully before using their vote. The media (sometimes known as the press) helps citizens to make up their minds about issues such as the Manchester congestion charge. It does this in the following ways:

- By providing facts on TV, on the internet or in newspapers. the media helps citizens to find out what is going on. Information in the press or media also helps citizens to form their own opinions.
- By interviewing people with different opinions on an issue and giving them publicity.
- By promoting the opinion of the media company or newspaper on a particular issue.

The UK is a democracy. In a democracy, the press or media are free to express any point of view as long as it is not **libellous** and does not encourage people to be racist or to engage in crime. This freedom is summed up by the term **free press**.

In a dictatorship, the government controls the media. The government of a dictatorship decides what information and opinions citizens will be allowed to see and hear. This means that citizens often do not have enough information to make up their own minds on an issue. Citizens in a dictatorship do not get the chance to see or hear other opinions on an issue.

A free press also has other important responsibilities in a democracy.
- It investigates any problems or injustices and lets citizens know about them.
- It exposes any wrong-doing by pressure groups, political parties or politicians.
- It protects and promotes the interests of people who are victims of injustice.
- It reminds citizens about promises made by politicians and shows whether these promises have been kept.
- It gives a fair hearing to different opinions.

How can citizens make decision-makers accountable for their actions?

In a democracy, there are several ways in which citizens can let decision-makers know if they are unhappy or want something to change. Meetings, letters and emails, petitions and protests all play a part in drawing attention to a citizen's point of view.

Of course, a campaign is likely to be more effective if large groups support the cause or if people set up a pressure group to organise and run the campaign. Gaining publicity is important so that more people hear about the campaign and find out how they can get involved. Elected politicians are more likely to listen to large groups. After all, people in the campaign group all have a vote and politicians are out of a job unless people vote for them in elections.

There is lots of evidence that politicians and civil servants do listen carefully to public opinion. On relatively non-controversial issues such as the RSPCA's lobbying on the welfare of laboratory animals (page 45) or even the *Daily Mirror*'s asbestos campaign (page 47), citizens and pressure groups are often successful.

When the media exposes politicians for having done something wrong, these politicians are often under great pressure to resign. If they remain as MPs or members of the Government, there is a risk that the reputation of Parliament or the Government will be damaged. However, on some occasions politicians stay in their job in spite of criticism. In 2009 Home Secretary Jacqui Smith was criticised for her expenses claims. This was headline news, but she refused to resign, saying that she had made some small mistakes but had done nothing wrong.

There are also examples where the UK Government has seemed to ignore both public opinion and widespread public protest. The wars in Iraq and Afghanistan were unpopular with the public but the Government continued with its policy in spite of protests.

A referendum gives citizens real power to make a decision on a major issue. There are very few referendums in representative democracies because many politicians feel that, once elected, it is their job to make decisions. The last national referendum in the UK was in 1975, when people voted in favour of joining the European Community (now the European Union). There have been more recent important referendums in Wales, Scotland and Northern Ireland on how government should be organised in those countries. Local referendums are allowed on any issue and can be asked for by small groups of voters. However, local politicians do not have to take notice of the results of the referendum.

Anti-war demonstrations took place across the UK in 2002 but the Government still invaded Iraq.

Having read this section, it is important that you decide for yourself how far citizens can hold decision-makers to account. Remember that in a representative democracy, citizens can wait for an election and then vote for a different set of politicians.

Sample exam questions: Democracy and voting

Try these questions for the short-course exam (answers on pages 100–101).

11. Which description below best describes the way in which a representative democracy works? *(1 mark)*
   i. People vote for the important issues.
   ii. People vote for politicians who consult them regularly on how they should vote.
   iii. People vote for politicians who then use their judgement to decide how best to run the country.
   iv. Civil servants decide important issues and ask politicians for their advice.

12. Give one example of a UK political party. *(1 mark)*

13. State one responsibility of the Prime Minister. *(1 mark)*

14. Explain why people's human rights are likely to be under threat if they live in a non-democratic country. In your answer, you should:
   ● Describe the differences between democratic and non-democratic forms of government.
   ● Explain which human rights are likely to be under threat in a non-democratic country. *(4 marks)*

15. Evaluate the following viewpoint: 'Citizens can gain most influence over decision-making by joining a pressure group.' In your answer, you should:
   ● Explain why joining a pressure group can help a citizen gain more influence over decision-makers.
   ● Use evidence or examples to support the points you make;
   ● Describe other ways in which citizens can gain influence over decision-makers.
   ● Evaluate how far you agree that joining a pressure group is the way in which a citizen can 'gain more influence over decision-makers'. *(12 marks)*

What are the UK's economic relationships with Europe?

The United Kingdom (UK) is one of the ten largest economies in the world. The wealth of people in the UK depends on trade with the rest of the world, especially Europe. We sell things to people in other countries. These are known as exports. We can then afford to bring goods into the UK from other countries. These are known as imports.

In 2008 the value of the UK's exports was nearly £207 billion. Of these exports, 67 per cent went to countries in the European Union (EU). Companies trading in the UK usually have important business partners in Europe, or are part of a European or global group of companies. Examples include the oil company Shell, the chemical and pharmaceutical company Reckitt Benckiser, Barclays Bank and the motor company Jaguar–Land Rover.

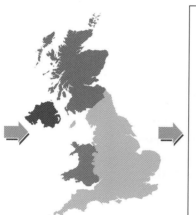

IMPORTS
- machinery
- oil
- motor vehicles
- electrical goods
- chemicals
- plastics
- clothing
- food

EXPORTS
- motor vehicles
- aircraft and engines
- machinery and equipment
- metals
- chemical products
- food and drink products
- oil and gas
- services (including banking and finance)

 The UK's main imports and exports.

Table G. The UK's top 20 trading partners in 2009	
Country	**% of trade**
USA	13
Germany	12
Netherlands	10
France	9
Ireland	8
Belgium	6
Italy	4
Spain	4
Sweden	2
Japan	1
Canada	1
United Arab Emirates	1
China	1
Singapore	1
Poland	1
Hong Kong	1
Switzerland	1
Australia	1
Denmark	1
India	1

What are the UK's political and legal relationships with Europe?

The UK has been part of the EU since 1975. The EU is an important political group of largely wealthy countries. In 2009 there were 27 countries in the EU, with others waiting to join. Membership of the EU determines many of the UK's political and legal relationships with other countries in Europe. UK representatives in the European Parliament help to decide treaties and laws, some of which then have to be adopted by the UK Parliament.

Origins of the European Union

After the Second World War (1939–1945) France and Germany decided that it was better to work together than to fight. They formed an alliance (joined forces) in 1951 along with four other countries. This alliance encouraged trade and co-operation and was the start of what we now know as the European Union (EU).

Most of the UK's trade is with countries in the European Union. Find the UK's major European trading partners on this map.

Legend:
- Member States
- Candidate Countries

Aims of the EU

The original aim of the EU was to prevent further war in Europe by bringing the European nations together into a co-operative alliance. EU member countries have more power in the world as a group than they could on their own. EU members can take joint action to help solve problems around the world. The EU also aims to promote human rights and democracy in all its member countries and across the world.

The EU aims to bring the laws and systems of each member country closer together (integration). This makes it easier for people to move between countries and for businesses to trade. By 2003 most of the member countries were using the same unit of currency (the euro) and working towards integration of such things as interest rates and tax levels. The UK Government decided not to introduce the euro and still has an independent economic policy. Many people in the UK are against greater integration and some wish to withdraw from the EU.

What are the UK's cultural relationships with Europe?

Cultural and sporting links have helped to bring the people of mainland Europe and the UK together in friendship. This has helped to promote communication and understanding between countries that were enemies and rivals for hundreds of years.

Most UK towns and cities, and some villages, have twinning links with similar communities in Europe. For example, the people of East Grinstead in West Sussex founded a town-twinning association in 1962. The town is now linked with five European towns: Bourg-de-Péage (France),

Mindelheim (Germany), Sant Feliu de Guixols (Spain), Schwaz (Austria) and Verbania (Italy). People in the different communities visit and get to know each other. They also participate in joint events such as sports, concerts and conferences. Twinning associations also encourage the study of foreign languages in schools.

Links between UK and European schools, universities, art galleries, museums and even zoos have enabled expertise to be shared and have led to a vast range of joint projects and activities. Some examples are given below.

- The EU's Socrates and Erasmus exchange programmes enable UK university students to spend part of their time studying at a European university. In one such university link, students from the University of Hull can spend time at the University of Murcia in south-eastern Spain.
- Eighteen European zoos are co-operating in an endangered species breeding programme for the Asiatic lion.
- The Tate Gallery's exhibition on futurism in 2009 borrowed exhibits from other art galleries across Europe.

Perhaps the most prominent links between the UK and Europe are connected with sport. A European golf team contests the Ryder Cup each year with the USA, while the Champions' League brings together the best European soccer teams and the Six Nations European rugby championship brings Italy and France into a competition to play the nations of the UK.

? Which communities are your village, town or city linked with? What joint events have happened or are planned?

What is the impact of EU decisions on citizens of the UK?

How are decisions made in the EU?

There are three decision-making bodies within the EU. Each has a different role but also has important links with the other two bodies. The system is complex because each government of the 27 member states expects to have a say.

New laws and regulations are proposed by the European Commission. The democratically elected European Parliament has to approve proposals put forward by the European Commission. Member states also have their say through the Council of the European Union.

Decisions made by the EU have an increasingly important impact on UK citizens.

COUNCIL OF THE EUROPEAN UNION

- The Council of the European Union is the main EU decision-making body. It represents the interests of the 27 individual member states.
- Each member state is represented by ministers from its own democratically elected government.
- The presidency of the Council is shared between member states – each member state has the presidency for six months.

Proposes new laws

Appoints commissioners

The Council and the Parliament work together on the main decisions

EUROPEAN COMMISSION

- The European Commission proposes new laws to the Council and Parliament.
- The Commission manages the introduction and enforcement of EU laws.
- Commissioners are appointed on a five-yearly basis by the Council in agreement with member states.
- The Commission is answerable to the European Parliament.

Proposes new laws

Parliament has to approve proposals made by the Commission

EUROPEAN PARLIAMENT

- The Members of the European Parliament (MEPs) are elected every five years by EU citizens.
- Parliament approves and checks the EU budget.
- Parliament considers Commission proposals on new laws.
- Parliament works with the Council on the main decisions.

Below are some examples of decisions made by the EU in 2008 and 2009:

- Two of the UK's biggest car-makers were given large loans to help them design and build a more environmentally friendly type of car.
- Patients in the UK and throughout the EU were allowed to shop around Europe for the best and quickest medical treatment.
- Performing rights fees for musicians were simplified to assist the development of satellite, cable and internet broadcasting, and to give listeners more choice.
- Trading standards were tightened up so that consumers across Europe could expect a similar standard when buying products such as fruit.

The European Parliament is made up of MEPs elected in each of the 27 member states.

What are the benefits and costs of the UK's membership of the EU?

Table H. Benefits and costs of EU membership

BENEFITS

Study, work and residence
EU citizens can live, work, study and retire in any EU country. More than two million young people have used EU programmes to study or train in another European country.

Travel and shopping
Citizens can travel across most of the EU without a passport and without border checks. They can shop in any other EU country without restrictions or additional taxes, as long as what they buy is for their own use.

The environment
EU member states have taken joint action to cut pollution. Europe's rivers and beaches are cleaner, vehicles pollute less and there are strict rules for waste disposal. A long-term energy strategy is being developed, because oil and gas reserves in EU countries are being used up.

Freedom, security and justice for all
EU citizens have equal access to justice everywhere in the EU. To tackle cross-border crime and terrorism, police and customs officers, immigration services and law courts co-operate in all EU countries.

Jobs and growth
The EU has removed barriers to trade and set European standards that all products must meet. This has helped make it easier to do business across Europe.

Peace and stability
War between EU countries is now unthinkable, thanks to the unity that has been built up between them over the last 50 years. The EU is now working to spread peace and stability beyond its borders.

COSTS

Democracy and decision-making
There is a danger that the UK will lose further important powers to the EU. This makes decision-making more remote from UK citizens and threatens our freedom to make decisions.

Public opinion
In a 2008 opinion poll, 65 per cent of people agreed that 'The EU is out of touch with normal people'. It is not good for democracy for the UK to remain a member of the EU if so many people are against it.

Paying out
Membership of the EU is expensive for a wealthy country like the UK. Costs will increase as greater numbers of poorer European countries join. Money from UK taxes is being used to help the poorer countries of Europe.

The UK's status as an independent nation
The UK is a major world economic, military and diplomatic power and has the world's most widely-used language. The UK government can negotiate with other countries more quickly and flexibly without the EU.

Trade and prosperity
There is a danger that membership of the EU will limit the UK's trade with the rest of the world and cause it to miss out on opportunities to do business with India and China.

Regulations and delay
The EU imposes thousands of regulations each year, many of which people feel are not necessary. With 27 countries involved, important decisions are often delayed.

What is the British Commonwealth?

Around 150 years ago, the UK was the most powerful country in the world. It had a huge **empire** that included large parts of the Americas, Africa and Asia. Australia and New Zealand were also part of the British Empire. To create this empire the British overthrew the existing rulers of a country and took charge. The British Empire was ruled from London and made the UK a very wealthy country.

English was, and still is, an international language spoken across the world. Many people from the UK emigrated to the 'new' lands (**colonies**) overseas while some people from the colonies moved to the UK (see page 19).

During the nineteenth and twentieth centuries, the colonies gradually gained independence, breaking away from UK control. This was almost always done peacefully. Many of these former colonies wanted to keep the trading and cultural links they had with one another and with the UK. So they formed the British Commonwealth, with the Queen at its head. At first, countries of the Commonwealth had important trade links with one another. However, the significance of these links has declined, especially following the UK's decision to join the EU in 1975.

The modern Commonwealth is a 'family' of 53 developed and developing nations around the world. It is a voluntary association of independent states that include many religions, races, languages and cultures.

Key terms

Empire A group of countries under the rule of a single person or state. In the British Empire, for example, Canada, India and large parts of Africa were ruled from London.

Colonies Those countries that are part of an empire. For example, Canada and India were British colonies.

The Commonwealth has an important role in promoting cultural understanding and the exchange of ideas. It encourages links between people, shares ideas between countries, encourages democracy and promotes **economic development**.

The Commonwealth Games, held every four years, brings the 'family' together in sporting competition. India was the host nation for the 2010 Commonwealth Games.

The major Commonwealth countries. Altogether there are 53 Commonwealth nations. They are developed or developing countries that have historical ties to the UK.

How does the United Nations (UN) help to resolve international conflict?

What is the United Nations (UN)?

The largest international organisation to which the UK belongs is the United Nations (UN). The UN was established in 1945 by 51 countries committed to preserving peace through international co-operation. Today, nearly every nation in the world belongs to the UN. There are almost 200 member countries.

Member countries agree to accept the **UN Charter**, an international treaty that sets out basic principles of international relations. According to the Charter, the UN has four purposes:

1 To maintain international peace and security.
2 To develop friendly relations among nations.
3 To co-operate in solving international problems.
4 To promote respect for human rights.

The United Nations is not a world government and it does not make laws. All the member countries have a voice and a vote.

Key terms

Economic development
Building up a country's ability to produce things that other people want to buy.

UN Charter A charter is a document that sets out the purpose of an organisation and the rights it expects members to promote. The UN Charter on Human Rights sets out the human rights that member countries are expected to follow.

Resolving disagreement and conflict

The United Nations aims to encourage all nations to agree international laws and treaties so that disputes can be avoided. Agreements on limiting the spread of nuclear weapons, care for the environment (see page 87) and the use of the sea have proved particularly tricky for the UN to negotiate because different national governments often have very different views.

In spite of reaching agreements in advance on some tricky international issues, there are often disputes between nations. These disputes are often about land or resources. The UN's **International Court of Justice**, based in The Hague (Netherlands), tries to settle such disputes. In 2009 the court dealt with several disputes about territory, including an argument between Costa Rica and Nicaragua over navigation rights at sea and another between Ukraine and Romania about claims to parts of the Black Sea. The **UN General Assembly** elects fifteen judges, each of whom serves on the court for nine years. This system avoids accusations of bias.

Where people are at risk of violence or where nations need support in making peace agreements work, the UN may agree to send a **peacekeeping mission**. The mission's job is to make sure that any peace treaty is upheld, that any former fighters follow international humanitarian law (see page 28) and that elections take place to select a new government.

The first UN peacekeeping mission was set up in 1948, when the **UN Security Council** sent military observers to the Middle East to monitor the ceasefire between Israel and its Arab neighbours. Since then, there have been a total of 63 UN peacekeeping missions around the world. In some cases UN soldiers will be prepared to fight in order to protect the rights of people at risk, but the priority is for peacekeeping forces to act without violence if possible.

In more extreme cases, the UN Security Council can apply **sanctions** to a national government. This means, for example, that other governments refuse to supply weapons to or trade with the government judged to be in the wrong. For example, sanctions were applied to Iraq when it invaded Kuwait in 1990.

Why does the UK follow UN agreements on human rights, international relations and the environment?

The UK government has long been an active and committed member of the United Nations. This commitment is strong because the UK is one of the five permanent members of the UN Security Council. (The other members are France, the USA, Russia and China.) This gives the UK considerable power because the UN Security Council makes important strategic decisions about global security.

Ten other countries are elected to be non-permanent members of the Security Council by all the member states at the General Assembly. These countries are elected for two years. In 2009 the ten non-permanent

Key terms

International Court of Justice Also known as the World Court, the International Court of Justice was set up by the United Nations to settle legal disputes between countries so as to avoid conflict between them.

Peacekeeping mission An attempt by a country or group of countries, such as the United Nations, to send armed forces to another country to prevent fighting and settle a dispute.

Sanctions Penalties that are imposed on a country by other countries in order to encourage that country to change its policies. For example, Commonwealth countries cut their trade with Zimbabwe to encourage its government to extend human rights.

UN General Assembly A meeting of all the member countries of the United Nations. It decides the policies and budget of the United Nations as well as appointing the non-permanent members to the Security Council.

UN Security Council The UN body that carries out the policy of the General Assembly by maintaining international peace and security. The Security Council can start peacekeeping operations, impose sanctions and organise military action.

members were Austria, Burkina Faso, Costa Rica, Croatia, Japan, Libya, Mexico, Turkey, Uganda and Vietnam.

The values of the UK Government, particularly its support for democracy, (see page 12) and the UK's dependency for its prosperity on world trade, also help to explain why UK governments are keen to support UN agreements.

How effective is the UN in resolving international conflicts and emergencies?

The International Court of Justice and UN peacekeeping missions have the respect and support of most governments across the world. This means that the work of the UN is often successful, as long as all sides in a conflict are ready to make peace. However, in 2009, there were some governments, such as Iran and North Korea, that did not respect the UN because they felt that the USA, the UK and France had far too much power.

Another problem arises when the UN attempts to intervene where a rebellion is taking place against a government or where a terrorist organisation is operating. In such cases, it is unlikely that the groups

A success story? – the United Nations mission in Liberia

Civil war in Liberia claimed the lives of almost 150,000 people – mostly civilians – and led to a complete breakdown of law and order. It resulted in some 850,000 people seeking refuge in neighbouring countries. Fighting began in 1989 between government forces and fighters who claimed membership of an opposition group called the National Patriotic Front of Liberia (NPFL), led by Charles Taylor (a former government official).

After a short period of peace, the civil war restarted in 2003. The United Nations established a peacekeeping mission (UNMIL) in Liberia through a Resolution (decision) of the UN Security Council (Resolution 1509). UNMIL's job was to support a ceasefire agreement and the peace process, to protect civilians and to support human rights. The mission also set out to improve national security in Liberia to prevent further conflict. This included national police training and the formation of a new, reorganised national army. Up until 2009 soldiers and police officers from nearly 50 nations, including the UK, had contributed UNMIL, and 126 UNMIL staff had been killed. In 2009 almost 12,000 peacekeepers were working in Liberia. Numbers were gradually being reduced, because the mission was going well.

An opinion poll of Liberian civilians in 2006 showed very positive support for the UN mission, with 91 per cent of people saying that they felt much safer. The UN was also praised for rebuilding roads and bridges, helping to supply fresh water and renovating schools and health centres. People reported that the UN had done a good job in retraining the police, but said that they still felt the police may not act fairly in the future. Civilians were also worried that the UN had not been able to deal with all the former fighters and there was concern that violence could restart if the UN left.

involved will follow international humanitarian law (see page 28) and the UN has much less power to use persuasion or sanctions. UN intervention is likely to be less effective in these cases.

The UN does not have its own army. Instead the Security Council asks UN member countries to contribute soldiers and civilians to peacekeeping missions. People from several nations are included in each mission, but this can lead to problems in leadership and co-ordination.

The cost of UN peacekeeping missions is over £3 billion per year, but mission commanders have sometimes been concerned about the time it takes to obtain further support from the UN when it is needed. When a nation's army is at war, no expense is spared to support an army and decisions are taken very quickly. In a UN peacekeeping mission, the commander has to ask for additional supplies and reinforcements. His or her requests have to be discussed and agreed by UN officials or even by the Security Council. This can take a long time, and the delays can put the success of a mission at risk.

Sample exam questions: The United Kingdom and the wider world

Try these questions for the short-course exam (answers on pages 101–102).

16. Which two countries below are members of the Commonwealth?
  i. Canada.
  ii. France.
  iii. Spain.
  iv. South Africa. *(1 mark)*

17. State one aim of the European Union (EU). *(1 mark)*

18. State one way in which the United Nations tries to resolve conflict. *(1 mark)*

19. Explain why some people might think that the UK should stop being a member of the EU. In your answer, you should:
  ● Give examples of the disadvantages of EU membership.
  ● Explain why people might feel strongly about at least one of these disadvantages. *(4 marks)*

20. Evaluate the following viewpoint: 'The United Nations (UN) is a waste of money.' In your answer, you should:
  ● Explain why the UN was set up.
  ● Describe what the UN does.
  ● Use evidence or examples to support the points you make.
  ● Evaluate how far you agree that 'the UN is a waste of money'. *(12 marks)*

3.1 Rights and responsibilities in school, college and the wider community

What moral rights do people have at home, school or college?

People in a family do not usually have to follow written rules. Instead, the way we behave in families is governed by the expectations we have of one another. Children expect parents to help and support them. Children feel they have a right to such support. Parents expect children to help around the house. Here too, parents feel they have a right to be helped with the housework. When a parent or child's expectations are not met, there are likely to be arguments because people feel let down.

There are more likely to be written rules in school or college, but informal expectations are just as important at school as in a family. Students expect teachers to teach lessons that are interesting and well organised. Students therefore feel they have a right to interesting and well-organised lessons. Teachers expect students to listen to instructions. Teachers therefore feel that they have a right to be listened to in class.

These are not *legal* rights, but **moral rights**. There is no law against not listening to a teacher. However, if students do not listen, then classroom relationships break down and students will make little progress.

Fill in the blanks in the grid below to show the moral rights of teachers, parents and students in your school or college.

Moral rights of students	Moral rights of teachers	Moral rights of parents
1. To have work handed back on time	1. To have the resources needed to teach good lessons	1. To be contacted in cases of misbehaviour
2.	2.	2.
3.	3.	3.

What moral responsibilities do people have at school or college?

We expect to have certain rights in our family and our school. Moral rights come with **moral responsibilities**. For example, it isn't fair for us to expect to be listened to unless we exercise the responsibility to listen to others.

Key terms

Moral responsibilities What we should do to support others so that they can enjoy certain rights. For example, students have a responsibility to make sure that their behaviour does not interfere with others' right to learn.
Moral rights What we expect from others in certain contexts. For example, parents expect to be contacted by teachers if their son or daughter misbehaves. This is not a legal right but parents still expect it to happen. Therefore it is a moral right – based on what can be reasonably expected in a school context.

Most schools have a **home–school agreement**. This sets out the rights and responsibilities of students, teachers and parents. A typical agreement might include responsibilities like those below.

Teachers' responsibilities	Parents' or carers' responsibilities	Students' responsibilities
Teach good lessons and set suitable class work and homework that will be marked regularly and returned promptly.	Check their son or daughter's homework timetable and diary. Take an interest in the work their children do at home and make sure it is completed.	Listen to teachers and work hard. Write all homework tasks in their diary and hand it in on time.

To check your understanding of rights and responsibilities of students in school, fill in the gaps in the grid below.

Moral right	Moral responsibility
To have work handed back on time	
	To speak out against bullying
To have personal property respected	
	To help anyone who is upset
To work in clean, tidy rooms	

What legal rights do people have at school or college?

Most of us get on well with others in our homes and at school. We understand our rights and responsibilities and can sort out any disagreements quickly.

Sometimes people do not carry out their responsibilities properly. Students, teachers or parents may feel that their rights have been ignored or infringed. If this happens, they may be able to use the law to protect themselves or help settle disputes.

There are hundreds of laws and regulations governing education and protecting the rights of students, teachers, parents and **school governors**. Other **legal rights** that apply in schools include the list on the next page.

Key terms

Home–school agreement A written agreement that sets out the rights and responsibilities of teachers, students and parents in a school or college.

Legal rights Expectations that the law says must be met. For example, we expect to be educated in a safe classroom. This is a legal right. If we are injured because a classroom is unsafe, we have a legal right to compensation.

School governor School governors have responsibility for choosing a head teacher, deciding school policies and making sure the school has high standards. Parents, teachers, students and others such as local business people can become school governors.

- All students have a right to receive religious education in school.
- All students have a right to receive sex education as well as to learn about the importance of marriage for family life.
- Teachers have the right to punish students for poor behaviour on the way to and from school.
- Teachers have the right to insist that a school uniform is worn, as long as the uniform regulations of the school are reasonable.
- Teachers have the right to search a student who they think may be carrying a knife.
- Students have a right to receive their education free of charges except for optional trips, music tuition, etc.

Case Study: Whose rights have been infringed?

Harry is thirteen and has special needs. He pushes to the front of the lunch queue as he is very hungry. A teacher asks him to go to the back of the queue. Harry refuses. It is not the first time Harry has disobeyed teachers. The teacher reports Harry to the head teacher. Without meeting with Harry, the head teacher immediately excludes him from school.

Other students
They have a moral right to expect that everyone should take their fair turn in the queue.

Following a suggestion from the Student Council, school prefects are on duty to help organise the lunch queue.

The teacher
He or she has a moral right to expect students to follow instructions.

The school's behaviour policy is very clear. Students can be excluded from the school for persistent disobedience.

Harry
He has a legal right to have his special needs taken into account before a decision is made about how to punish him. He has a legal right to make a statement to the head teacher before the head decides what action to take.

In this case, legal rights have been ignored. Harry's parents can complain to the school governors. If this doesn't work, they can take legal action. The head teacher will have to allow Harry to return to school.

What other action do you think the head should take?

Activity

The law helps to protect and regulate the rights of students, teachers, parents and governors in schools and colleges.

Which of the examples below do you think are legal rights?

- Teachers can use reasonable force against a student.
- Parents can withdraw their child from sex education lessons.
- Teachers can keep students in detention even if a parent objects.
- Parents can choose a school for their children.
- Students can see their school records.
- Parents must receive at least one report on their child's progress each year

Answers on page 102.

What legal responsibilities do people have at school or college?

Parents have a legal responsibility for their children's education and behaviour. The Education Act 1996 gives parents a legal responsibility to make sure that their children have a proper full-time education. This education does not have to be in a school. Parents are able to provide education at home as long as it is 'efficient' and suitable for the age and ability of their child. Parents who fail to ensure that their child has a proper education may be fined or imprisoned.

If parents cannot agree which school their child should go to, the decision may have to be made by the courts. In such cases, the court must listen to the wishes of the child involved.

In cases where a student is excluded from school, parents must keep their child away from the school grounds and other public places. Failure to do this might lead to a fine.

Parents whose child often misbehaves in school can be given a Parenting Order to help them carry out their responsibilities in dealing with their child's behaviour. Parenting Orders may mean that parents have to attend special classes to improve their parenting skills.

Read the extract from the BBC News website below to decide how far legal action against parents has helped to improve school attendance. What other action do you think may be needed?

Truancy jailing every two weeks
by Sean Coughlan and James Westhead

From BBC News website (news.bbc.co.uk), 12 February 2009

A parent is jailed for their child's truancy once a fortnight. Since 2002, penalties for parents have risen rapidly, with prosecutions in England up 76 per cent.

Despite the penalties, unauthorised absences are higher than in 1997. The latest figures on tackling truancy and parental responsibility show that there has been a 41 per cent annual increase in the number of Parenting Orders to improve attendance.

'It's important that we back schools and local authorities in using these powers to tackle problem absentees and bad behaviour, they rightly make parents take responsibility for their children,' says England Children's Minister Delyth Morgan.

The legal responsibilities of teachers

Teachers have a legal responsibility to act as careful parents would towards their own children of a similar age. This means that teachers and head teachers sometimes have to make difficult decisions about what to do. For example, should students be allowed to throw snowballs, play rugby at break time without a qualified teacher on duty, eat their lunch in classroom without supervision, or make a teacher a cup of tea? Discuss these examples with your classmates and teacher.

How are legal rights and responsibilities reinforced and protected in schools?

Most legal rights and responsibilities in schools are protected and reinforced informally without the need to get school governors, lawyers or the police involved.

Copies of school rules are given to teachers, parents and students so that everyone is clear about their moral and legal rights and responsibilities. Most schools have copies of their policies on their website and parents can request paper copies if they need them. Many schools advertise expectations for behaviour on classroom noticeboards and in student diaries.

All schools should have a complaints policy. This policy sets out what parents and students should do if they are unhappy about something that has happened in school.

If students, parents or teachers are unhappy, they are usually asked to sort out the problem with the person responsible before taking any further action. However, if they are not satisfied, it is possible to make a formal, written complaint to the school governors or the local authority.

**The stages of a
school complaints policy**

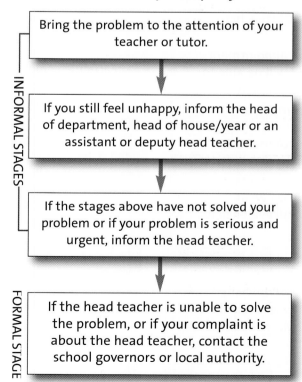

INFORMAL STAGES

Bring the problem to the attention of your teacher or tutor.

If you still feel unhappy, inform the head of department, head of house/year or an assistant or deputy head teacher.

If the stages above have not solved your problem or if your problem is serious and urgent, inform the head teacher.

FORMAL STAGE

If the head teacher is unable to solve the problem, or if your complaint is about the head teacher, contact the school governors or local authority.

An example: bullying

What the law says

Bullying is a form of harassment and may include assault. Harassment and assault are criminal offences.

All schools have a legal duty to make sure students are safe in school and on the way to and from school. All schools must, by law, have an anti-bullying policy.

The next section and the box below show the **informal action** that a parent could take if:

- their child has complained to them about bullying for the first time.
- a teacher has promised to deal with the bullying but it has happened again.

It also shows the **formal action** a parent can take if, for example, the head teacher has told them that that nothing can be done because the bullying has taken place on the way to school.

What can parents do if their child is being bullied at school?

If other students at the school are doing the bullying, the school has a legal responsibility to try to sort the problem out. All schools must have an anti-bullying policy.

- Parents should encourage their child to talk to their teacher or tutor.
- Parents can also contact the school and make an appointment to talk to someone. A teacher, tutor or year head will be able to help them decide the best way of sorting out the problem.
- Parents should discuss the problem and try to come to a resolution. If they feel the issue is not being dealt with effectively, they may need to contact a more senior member of staff.
- If the child tells their parents about being bullied, parents should keep a record of every incident, noting down what happened with dates and times. This will be useful evidence to take to the school if the bullying continues.

Taking legal action

Most parents are initially happy to let teachers deal with bullying problems, but if the bullying continues they may take more formal action. Bullying often involves harassment, assault, blackmail or the misuse of electronic media. These are all serious criminal offences, so students and their parents have the right to report bullying to the police.

The police have a right to investigate any bullying reported to them, and school staff have a legal responsibility to assist the police with any investigation.

Fairtown School policy

Bullying is unacceptable. We investigate all incidents that have taken place in school. We always give the bullies the chance to stop by pointing out the problem to them. We also contact their parents. Further bullying will lead to punishment. This can include detentions or fixed-term exclusion from school. If bullying persists, we may exclude a student permanently from school.

Key terms

Informal action This type of action is not placed on any record and usually will not involve any legal process. School governors, police or lawyers are unlikely to be involved. A break-time detention or a parent emailing a teacher to complain that work has not been marked are examples of informal action.

Formal action This is an action that is part of a legal process and is carefully recorded. The exclusion of a student from school is an example of formal action. There are strict national guidelines that head teachers have to follow. Parents have the right to ask school governors to review any decision.

Head teachers and governors have a legal responsibility to make sure schools are safe places for students and staff, as well as to have an anti-bullying policy and to take action quickly if bullying is reported. Students or their parents can take civil action against the school for failure to carry out these responsibilities.

How effective are local authorities and government departments at giving advice and support to citizens about their rights?

Local authorities have a responsibility to offer advice and support to citizens on such issues as housing, education, trading standards, transport and the availability of social care. The government has a responsibility to provide advice and support on such issues as taxation, benefits, pensions, the school curriculum, qualifications, energy saving,

How good is the West Sussex County Council Website at advising people about their rights in education?				
Statement	Tend to agree with statement	Website average on this measure	Tend to agree with counter-statement	Counter-statement
Directions from the home page were very clear	X			It was difficult to navigate through the website
People's rights were stated very clearly and linked to the Council's responsibilities			X	It was difficult to find a clear statement of people's rights
There was clear advice about how to protect and promote your rights		X		Advice did not exist, was confusing or unclear
There were good links to other helpful organisations		X		There were few worthwhile links

West Sussex County Council website – comments on the effectiveness of the advice available on education

The homepage was very crowded. However, if you knew that you wanted advice related to education, it was easy to navigate from the home page to the website section on education and then to a section called Information for Parents. From there, it was easy to find out how to make a complaint about a school but much harder to find out about your rights as a student or parent. Usually students and parents were advised to contact their school, but a contact number at the County Council was also provided. There were some useful links to government websites such as the Parents' Centre site which gives detailed advice to parents and students about education issues.

? Use a grid similar to the one on the left to evaluate the effectiveness of the information provided by a local authority or government department. The grid is based on an evaluation of West Sussex County Council's website for the quality of advice and support given to students and parents on rights in education. The evaluation is based on the website as it was in 2009. (The Council was aware of the problems of navigating the site and had a solution in hand.)

the law, justice and citizenship. In preparing for the exam, make sure that you have visited your local authority's website or the website of a government department.

The DirectGov website

This is the 'official government website for citizens'. It claims to give 'easy access to the public services you use and the information you need' with 'public services all in one place'.

Dealing with complaints

People who make complaints are sometimes still not happy with the response they receive. If this happens, people can contact organisations set up by the government to help in these situations. This may be an official regulator (see OFSTED below) – or an **ombudsman**, as in the case of the Health Ombudsman. There is a regulator, ombudsman or similar independent organisation to check on each public service and also for some essential privately-provided services such as water, gas, electricity and transport. Regulators and commissions have the power to investigate a complaint and help to resolve it. Although these organisations were set up by the government to safeguard standards in public services, they are independent (see OFSTED box below).

Go to the OFSTED website (www.ofsted.gov.uk) and find out how easy it is to make a complaint. Consider how easy it is to find advice about the action to take if you are unhappy with your school.

> **?** Find the DirectGov website (www.direct.gov.uk) and try it out. Use the evaluation grid on the previous page to decide how it measures up. Search for advice on education. Is the advice easy to find? Are rights and responsibilities set out clearly? Are there links to other useful sites that might offer you support?

> ## Key term
>
> **Ombudsman** An ombudsman checks to see whether people have been treated unfairly by looking into complaints about services they have used such as the National Health Service.

The Office for Standards in Education (OFSTED)

Extract adapted from the OFSTED website (www.ofsted.gov.uk)

We will report fairly and truthfully; listen to service users and providers; and communicate our findings to service providers and policy-makers.

We do not report to government ministers but directly to Parliament. This independence means you can rely on us for impartial information.

In education, OFSTED inspects schools regularly and makes recommendations about how schools can improve their service to students. Sometimes OFSTED will carry out a special inspection of a school in response to complaints from parents and students.

How effective are independent agencies at giving information and advice about citizens' rights?

Until recently, it was difficult for citizens to find clear information about their rights. This led to independent agencies being set up to help.

One of the best-known independent agencies is Citizens Advice. This is a charity funded by donations from businesses and members of the public.

There is a Citizens Advice Bureau in most large towns, where people can drop in when they have a problem or need information. Alternatively, people can phone or email. Trained volunteers provide most of this free advice and information.

Citizens Advice concentrates on advice about debt, benefits, housing, employment, immigration and consumer problems. It is also a pressure group. In 2008 Citizens Advice campaigned about the need to reduce the cost of school uniforms, because low-income families were having problems affording uniforms.

Try the Citizens Advice website (www.citizensadvice.org.uk). Is it easy to use? Is the advice helpful? How does it compare with the sites run by your local authority or the DirectGov website?

An independent source of advice for young adults is TheSite.org (www.thesite.org). It is owned and run by YouthNet UK, a charity founded in 1995. TheSite.org aims to be the first place all young adults turn to when they need support and guidance through life. Their philosophy is to provide young people with high-quality, impartial information and advice, and let them make their own decisions.

How are our human rights protected?

The basis of human rights is respect for each individual human life and for human dignity. Human rights do not have to be bought, earned or inherited. They belong to all of us simply because we are all human. We all have a responsibility to safeguard human rights and not to take them away from anyone.

The Universal Declaration of Human Rights 1948

After the Second World War ended in 1945, people felt it was important for the United Nations (UN) to draw up a Universal Declaration of Human Rights. This sets out the basic human rights and responsibilities for everyone. While these are not laws that each country must follow, the rights in the Declaration do help us to measure the human rights record of different governments across the world.

Article 1 of the Declaration states:
> 'All human beings are born free and equal in dignity and rights. They are endowed with reason and conscience and should act towards one another in a spirit of brotherhood.'

The other 29 Articles from the Declaration include the following.
- Everyone has a right to life, liberty and security. (Article 2)
- No one shall be subject to torture or degrading treatment or punishment. (Article 5)
- All are equal before the law. (Article 7)
- Everyone has a right to seek and enjoy, in other countries, asylum from persecution. (Article 14)
- Marriage shall be entered into only with the free and full consent of the intending spouses. (Article 16)
- Everyone has the right to freedom of opinion and expression. (Article 19)
- Everyone has a right to education. (Article 26)

Key facts about the Citizens Advice service

Compiled from information on the Citizens Advice website (www.citizensadvice.org.uk)

- The Citizens Advice service helps people resolve their money, legal and other problems by providing free advice and information, and by influencing policymakers.
- Citizens Advice is a registered charity.
- The service is run by a total of 26,000 people, 20,000 of whom are trained volunteers.
- Citizens Advice provides free, independent and impartial information and advice from over 3,200 locations. It helps people to resolve over 5.5 million problems every year.
- Citizens Advice also co-ordinates social policy, media, publicity and parliamentary work and maintains an information and advice website at www.adviceguide.org.uk, which receives over 7.3 million visits every year.

The European Convention on Human Rights 1950

The Council of Europe built on the Universal Declaration of Human Rights to produce the European Convention on Human Rights (ECHR) in 1950. European citizens can appeal to the European Court of Human Rights (ECtHR) if they feel that laws in their own country have not protected their rights.

The ECHR gives European citizens the following legal rights.
- Life, liberty and security of the person.
- A fair trial in civil and criminal matters.
- The right to vote and be a candidate in elections.
- Freedom of thought, conscience and religion.
- Freedom of expression.
- Property or peaceful enjoyment of possessions.
- Freedom of assembly and association.

The ECHR forbids:
- torture and inhuman or degrading treatment or punishment
- the death penalty
- slavery and forced labour
- discrimination in the enjoyment of rights included in the Convention.

The Human Rights Act 1998

In 1998 the UK government passed the Human Rights Act. This brought the articles of the ECHR into UK law. This means that UK courts can deal with people's claims that their human rights have been threatened.

Examples of cases brought to the European Court of Human Rights

- Torture and ill-treatment of prisoners.
- Telephone tapping.
- Discrimination against homosexuals.

Key terms

Abortion the termination (ending) of a pregnancy at an early stage, usually through a surgical operation.

Euthanasia The process of helping someone to die in a dignified way before they would normally do so.

The Human Rights Act – frequently asked questions

Q Does the Human Rights Act give people total freedom to do what they like?

A No. People can only enjoy their rights as long they do not restrict other people's freedoms. People have freedom of speech but must not lie about other people or abuse them. To do this would restrict the other person's human right to personal security.

Q If we have the Human Rights Act, is there any point in having other laws?

A The Human Rights Act provides a framework for many of our laws, but it is still up to Parliament to decide what should happen within this framework. The Human Rights Act states that all people should have the right to vote, but it does not fix a particular voting age. It is up to each country's Parliament to decide.

Q Does everyone have a right to freedom?

A No. There are rules to allow freedom to be taken away from criminals, people who may be planning to commit a criminal offence, people with infectious diseases and people trying to enter a country illegally.

Q If we have the Human Rights Act, why is there still heated debate about issues such as **abortion** and **euthanasia**?

A Sometimes rights clash. The right to life may clash with a parent's right to make choices. There are also debates about when life starts and when it stops. (At present abortions are not allowed after the 24th week of pregnancy because life is said to have started at that point. Euthanasia is illegal in the UK but legal in countries such as Switzerland and Australia.)

How effective is the Universal Declaration of Human Rights at protecting human rights across the world?

The UN's Universal Declaration of Human Rights has had a considerable influence on law across Europe and in the United Kingdom (see pages 26–27). People's rights enjoy a considerable level of protection as a result of the Universal Declaration. However, even in the UK, there are claims that people's human rights are restricted unreasonably because of fear of terrorism. (See page 29 and the BBC News website extract below.)

There are countries across the world where human rights have much less priority than in the UK. The pressure group Amnesty International was founded in 1961 to highlight human rights abuses worldwide. Amnesty was founded by lawyer Peter Benenson, after he read about two Portuguese students who had been sentenced to seven years in prison for raising their glasses in a toast to freedom.

Amnesty is still an active pressure group with thousands of supporters, many of whom take action to help protect human rights across the world. They do this in the following ways:

- Writing letters and sending emails to leading politicians protesting about unfair treatment of individuals.
- Publicising the cases of people who have been unfairly put in prison.
- Organising protests against particular governments.
- Persuading people not to go on holiday to or trade with the offending country.

Anti-terror tactics 'weaken law'

Adapted from the BBC News website (news.bbc.co.uk), 16 February 2009

Anti-terror measures worldwide have seriously undermined international human rights law, a report by legal experts says.

After a three-year global study, the International Commission of Jurists said many countries used the public's fear of terrorism to introduce measures such as detention without trial, illegal disappearance and torture.

It also said that the UK and the USA have 'actively undermined' international law by their actions.

The Commission said that the framework of international law that existed before the 9/11 attacks on the US was robust and effective. But now countries like the USA and the UK were undermining it.

Sample exam questions: Rights and responsibilities in school, college and the wider community

Try these questions for the full-course exam (answers on pages 102–103).

1. State one way in which rights are reinforced in schools.   *(1 mark)*

2. State one legal responsibility of teacher in a school.   *(1 mark)*

3. State three different rights that parents have.   *(3 marks)*

4. Study Document 1 below and answer the questions that follow.

Document 1. Ombudsman criticises Council over disabled homeless applicant

Adapted from the website of the Local Government Ombudsman (www.lgo.org.uk)

The London Borough of Redbridge failed to take sufficient account of a man's hearing disability when dealing with his homelessness application, finds Local Government Ombudsman Tony Redmond.

The Ombudsman finds that the Council was at fault for several reasons, including:

- Interviewing Mr Bennett without a British Sign Language (BSL) interpreter even though he cannot communicate without a BSL interpreter.
- Delaying unreasonably for 12 months the promised training for frontline staff on disability awareness.
- Failing to comply with the requirements of the Disability Discrimination Act to make 'reasonable adjustments' to enable disabled people to access services.

The Council has already paid Mr Bennett £750 for failing to provide an interpreter and a textphone facility. Council staff have now had Deaf Awareness Training and a textphone facility has been provided.

In addition, the Ombudsman also considers that the Council should:

- Pay Mr Bennett an additional £500 for the inconvenience.
- Remind all staff of the importance of recording service users' special communication needs and checking these records before attempting to contact them.
- Remind all staff of the importance of complying with its Interpretation and translation policy.

---

a. State one piece of evidence from Document 1 that shows that staff training was a problem for Redbridge Council. *(1 mark)*

b. State two ways in which Mr Bennett's complaint has been put right.
(2 marks)

c. Write a reasoned argument to oppose the viewpoint that, 'complaining about the actions of organisations that provide public services is difficult and usually a waste of time'. You must do the following in your answer:

- Explain key terms such as public services.
- Explain how a complaints process works.
- Use evidence to support your argument. *(6 marks)*

3.2 Rights and responsibilities as citizens within the economy and welfare systems

Why might the interests of employers and employees conflict?

Show the lists below to an employer, employee or both. How far do they agree with the lists of wants? What would they add? Which points do they think are most and least important?

Using the lists, identify at least two areas where the interests of employers and employees are similar, and two areas where they may clash.

What employees want

- An interesting job in a pleasant and safe environment.
- Good rates of pay and other benefits.
- A long-term contract with high levels of protection in case of illness or redundancy.
- To be consulted on changes within the business.
- Training to develop their skills.
- Chances for promotion.
- A secure pension.

What employers want

- Customers to be satisfied and to come back to order more goods or services.
- To keep sales up.
- To keep costs down.
- To keep quality up.
- Their prices to be competitive with other similar businesses.
- To produce products or services that continue to meet customers' needs.
- Workers who are well trained and motivated.
- Investors who receive a good return on their investment.
- To ensure that the business survives in bad times and grows in good times.

The boxed article that follows might help you. This shows how workers felt when the car maker BMW cut 850 jobs at its Oxford car plant.

Job cuts at Mini spark angry rows
Adapted from the BBC News website (news.bbc.co.uk) 16 February 2009

An employee, Javid Najibi, said he had been told to leave after four years at the plant and that he was likely to get no payout. 'It's bad news for everybody. There's no work any more for the weekend shift. No one knows about the future plans,' he said.

Worker Silvia Fernandes said: 'I've been here four years and I've never been sick, I've never missed work and they tell me one hour before that I've been sacked.'

The carmaker is the latest in a long line of car manufacturers in the UK to announce factory closures and redundancies for employees.

Key terms

Maternity leave Paid leave from work available to female workers who are expecting a baby. In 2009, 39 weeks of leave was granted for each pregnancy.

Paternity leave Paid leave from work for the partner of a women who gives birth. In 2009, workers had a right to two weeks of leave.

How does the law protect employers and employees?

Legal protection for employees

As long as your school gives you permission, you can get a job from the age of thirteen. There are limits on the type of work you can do. This is to protect your health and safety. Also:

- No more than two hours can be worked on any school day.
- No work can be done before 7a.m. or after 7p.m.

There are also legal safeguards on working hours and conditions for people aged sixteen and over. Also workers have legal rights to:

- regular rest breaks
- **maternity** and **paternity leave**
- paid holidays.

Other important legal rights include:

- The right to a written contract that explains such things as pay, conditions and the work to be done.
- The right to be treated equally, with no discrimination because of race, colour, nationality, religion, gender, marital status, sexual orientation, disability or age.
- Pay at, or above, the **national minimum wage**.
- The right to a healthy and safe workplace.
- The right to be given fair reasons for dismissal and, usually, a period of 'notice' before you have to leave.

Legal protection for employers

Employers have legal rights that enable them to take action against employees whose behaviour might damage the business. The actions they can take include official warnings, cuts in pay and even dismissal.

Employers have the right to expect that their employees should:

- Work skillfully, carefully and well.
- Be honest, obedient and not act against the employer's interests.
- Not disclose confidential information about the business.
- Take care of the employer's property.

Employers also have legal rights to any patents, discoveries or inventions that an employee makes during working hours.

Employers have other important legal rights. These include:

- The right to protection against other businesses that attempt to copy the employers' product or business idea (see also pages 78–79).
- By making their business a 'limited company', employers can take out business loans without placing their personal property at risk.

How might employers' interests conflict with the need to protect the environment?

Two of the most important goals for employers are to keep the costs of production down and to keep sales up.

These goals sometimes conflict with the needs of the environment. For example, it may be more costly for an employer to switch to environmentally friendly packaging. By switching, the employer may have to charge more for the product. With different packaging, the product may also look less attractive to the customer. As a result, sales may fall – something the employer may not want to risk.

The extract that follows overleaf suggests that UK supermarkets produce too much packaging, almost 40 per cent of which cannot be recycled. The Local Government Association (LGA) wants supermarkets to pay for the collection of their packaging as an incentive for them to cut back.

Key term

National minimum wage As long as they are aged sixteen or over, workers have the right to receive pay per hour at a rate set by the government or higher. In 2009 the minimum hourly rate for a sixteen-year-old was £3.53 per hour.

Pay recycling costs, stores told

Adapted from the BBC News website (news.bbc.co.uk), 17 February 2009

Packaging means greater use of landfill sites leading to higher council tax bills, the LGA said. A spokesperson said that less food packaging will help businesses as well as customers. 'When packaging is sent to landfill, it's costly for taxpayers and damaging for the environment. If supermarkets create unnecessary rubbish, they should pay for it to be recycled.'

A spokesperson for the supermarkets said: 'It's not fair to say that supermarkets use lots of needless packaging. Packaging reduces waste by protecting and preserving products. The biggest barrier to recycling is local authorities' failure to agree on which materials they're prepared to recycle.'

? Read the extract on the left, then consider why supermarkets use packaging, and why the Local Government Association (LGA) wants supermarkets to use less packaging and recycle more waste. Discuss with your friends and your teacher what action local authorities and government could take to encourage supermarkets to use less packaging and recycle more waste.

How does the Government use taxation and regulation to encourage environmentally responsible behaviour?

The Government and local authorities try to persuade citizens and businesses to behave in ways that protect and support the environment. Much of this persuasion is done through education and campaigning, but results are sometimes disappointing.

The boxes below show some examples of taxes and regulations that aim to encourage people to be more environmentally friendly.

Landfill tax

A tax paid for each tonne of waste deposited at landfill sites. Businesses can reduce the tax they pay by reusing and recycling more. Money from the tax is used to support environmentally friendly projects.

Air passenger duty

A special tax paid when you buy an airline ticket. In 2009 the extra tax on a flight to the USA was £20.

The tax is designed to discourage people from flying.

Climate change levy

A charge made to businesses with very large energy use. It raised £800 million in 2008.

The tax is designed to encourage businesses to cut down on energy use.

Fuel duty

A special tax paid on petrol and diesel fuel. In the UK, 72 per cent of the cost of each litre of fuel is to pay fuel duty and VAT (value-added tax).

Fuel duty is designed to encourage people to drive more fuel-efficient vehicles.

Vehicle excise duty (road tax)

An annual charge paid by people who have vehicles on the road. Environmentally friendly vehicles may pay nothing. Vehicles with high CO_2 emissions paid as much as £400 road tax in 2009.

Congestion charge

A fee paid by drivers each time they take their vehicle into central London. Motorcycles, buses, taxis and environmentally friendly vehicles pay nothing. The tax is designed to reduce traffic and encourage people to use public transport so that pollution is cut.

As part of the United Nations Kyoto Agreement of 1997, the UK Government agreed to cut emissions of carbon dioxide. Since then the Government and local authorities have brought in more taxes and regulations to encourage citizens and businesses to behave in ways that cause less damage the environment.

There have been protests against some of the environmentally friendly taxes listed on the previous page. People have sometimes found them hard to afford. In 2000 and again in 2008 motorists protested against the high tax on fuel by blocking roads and stopping petrol tankers leaving oil refineries. This direct action help to persuade the Government to shelve plans to increase fuel duty.

How do trade unions support and represent their members?

Trade unions were set up by groups of employees to protect workers' rights and to campaign for fair wages. If people are members of a trade union and have been treated unfairly by employers, they can ask their union for advice and help.

Trade unions also negotiate with employers over pay and conditions for their members. They act as a pressure group on government to gain better rights for all employees.

Many trade unions support and donate money to the Labour Party. The Labour Party was founded by the trade unions in 1900 in order to elect working people as Members of Parliament (MPs). Many Labour MPs in Parliament are still supported by particular trade unions.

Supporting members – services provided by trade unions

As well as legal advice, trade unions provide a wide range of services to their members. These include the following.
- Representation at work. (A trade union official will accompany and advise people who need to discuss a complaint or disciplinary matter with their boss.)
- Education and training. (Most trade unions run training courses to help their members learn new skills. Some unions even help members financially if they want to go to university.)
- A benevolent fund. (Most trade unions can offer financial help to their members if they have a major life crisis.)

How do employers' associations support and represent their members?

Employees can join trade unions for advice and support. Employers also have organisations that they can join for a similar purpose.

Two of the largest and best known employers' associations are the Federation of Small Businesses (FSB) and the Confederation of British Industry (CBI). The FSB and CBI are both able to offer legal advice to employers and have regular discussions with the Government to promote policies to help businesses. Both of these employers' associations are keen to limit the amount of tax paid by employers and to reduce the number of regulations affecting business.

Supporting business – some services provided by employers' associations

Other services provided to their members by the FSB and CBI include:

- Legal documents online to save employers time in drawing up policies, contracts and official letters.
- Financial advice to help with loans, overdrafts, leasing and insurance.
- Business support to help with such things as checking customers' ability to pay and selling products overseas.

FSB and CBI campaigns

Like the trade unions, the FSB and CBI organise campaigns to promote the interests of business. Examples of campaigns include:

- Delaying new employment and environmental protection laws that would be expensive for business.
- Giving businesses relief from local government taxation (business rates) during the recession of 2009.

Why are patent and copyright laws important for business?

What is patent law?

A patent gives a citizen the legal right to stop others from copying, making, selling or importing an invention without permission.

The existence of a patent may be enough on its own to stop others from trying to exploit an invention. If this does not work, the patent holder has the right to take legal action to stop the invention being exploited by someone else. The patent holder can also claim damages.

A patent also allows the person holding it to:

- Sell the invention and all the intellectual property (IP) rights.
- License the invention to someone else but retain all the IP rights.
- Discuss the invention with others in order to set up a business based around the invention.

The public also benefits from patents because the Government's Intellectual Property Office (IPO) publishes each patent after eighteen months. Others can then gain advance knowledge of technological developments that they will eventually be able to use freely once the patent ceases.

The British inventor James Dyson used patent law to stop other businesses copying his bagless vacuum cleaner.

What if someone does not patent their invention?

If an invention is not patented, anyone can use, make or sell the invention without permission. People can attempt to keep their invention secret, but this may not be possible for a product where the technology is on display.

What is copyright law?

Copyright applies to a wide range of written and recorded material, including books, magazines, software, drawings and photographs.

The Copyright Designs and Patent Act (1988) does not protect ideas for a work. It is only when the work itself is produced – for example when a piece of music or a book is published – that copyright automatically protects it. People do not have to apply for copyright as they do for a patent.

A work protected by copyright can have more than one copyright. For example, an album of music can have separate copyrights for individual songs, sound recordings and artwork. Copyright law is complex and cases can take years to sort out. In the Procul Harem case study (right), the court case reported in the *Mirror* newspaper was not the end of the story. The decision of the High Court was reversed in the Court of Appeal. Then, three years after the first court case, the matter was considered by the House of Lords.

Why is it important for businesses to be socially responsible?

A business does not exist in isolation. It is part of a community. Employees and their families depend on the business they work for. Customers, suppliers and the local community are all affected by what businesses do. The way in which a business makes its products and services also has an impact on the environment.

Corporate Social Responsibility (CSR) takes all this into account. CSR means taking a responsible attitude to all those who work for the business and are affected by it. CSR means that a business will behave in an ethical manner by trying to bring benefits to other people as well as making a profit.

CSR offers business benefits. A business with a reputation for being a good employer, supporting the community and caring about the environment will be more popular with the public. Workers who feel valued by their employer will work harder and more effectively. Other businesses will favour partnerships with companies with high levels of CSR, because it will be good for their reputation. In these ways, socially responsible businesses can be more successful and therefore more profitable.

Lighter shade of pale for Procul Harem star

Adapted from the website of the Mirror *newspaper, (www.mirror.co.uk), 20 December 2006*

PROCUL Harem singer Gary Brooker today lost a High Court copyright action over the group's 1967 hit 'A Whiter Shade of Pale'. Voted one of the greatest pop songs of all time, 'A Whiter Shade of Pale' sold more than 10 million records and still earns huge sums in royalties.

Former band member Matthew Fisher claimed he was due 50 per cent of the song's royalties because of his contribution to the song.

Today Fisher was awarded a 40 per cent share of the musical copyright but his claim for back royalties, which could have amounted to more than £1 million, was rejected.

Mr Justice Blackburne said Fisher's contribution to 'A Whiter Shade of Pale' was 'significant' but not as substantial as that of Brooker, who now faces a large share of the legal costs (up to £500,000).

Evaluating CSR in a business

Businesses can check their level of CSR by finding out:
- The percentage of customers who use the business more than once.
- Levels of customer satisfaction and customer complaints.
- Energy consumption.
- Levels of waste, and amount of recycling.
- Levels of staff absence.
- Quality of staff training.
- Number of grievances raised by staff.
- The value of business support to the community as a percentage of profits.

How does the government help to manage the economy?

The term 'economy' is used to describe all the business activity and wealth creation that takes place in a country. If the economy is 'booming', there is a large amount of business activity, people have jobs and we tend to have money to spend on things we want.

In a booming economy it is easy to borrow money, as the banks are confident that people will be able to pay back their loans. People use the borrowed money to buy even more goods, leading to higher levels of business activity and more jobs.

When business activity declines, people often lose their jobs. They might be unable to pay back their loans, and even banks can go out of business. People have less money to spend and start saving more in case they become unemployed. As people spend less, demand for products falls, businesses fail and people lose their jobs. The economy is in 'recession'.

One of the main ways any government manages the economy is to encourage business activity.

When businesses are doing well, a government might increase taxes so that it can afford to build new schools, hospitals and roads. The government will want to make sure that the economy doesn't grow too rapidly, or lending might get out of control and prices may increase. Both of these can damage economic activity in the long term.

Where businesses are doing badly, a government might want to support them with new loans so that they can invest in new products and equipment. A government might also cut taxes so that people can spend more of their money on goods and services – so giving businesses a welcome sales boost and encouraging them to employ more workers.

Adjusting the economy

Governments try to adjust economic activity in their country by making changes to taxes, interest rates, pensions or bank activity. The diagram on page 81 shows some examples of how changing these items can affect economic activity.

Triodos Bank

Triodos Bank is based on strong ethical principles. It only lends to and invests in organisations that create real social or environmental value such as charities, ethical businesses and environmental projects. Since 2006 Triodos has run an annual Women in Ethical Business Award, to recognise and highlight the work of women running ethical businesses.

TAXES

VAT cut by 2.5%.

You have more money to spend!

INTEREST RATES

Increased by 1%.

Loans are more expensive. Sales of houses and cars fall.

PENSIONS

Extra £60 per year for all pensioners

Food and energy sales go up

BANKS

Government makes sure banks have more money to lend

Business activity increases

Ways in which government action can affect the economy.

What public services do the Government and local authorities provide?

There are some services that it would be difficult for businesses to provide on their own. For example, a private business may have difficulty running a public service like the army or being responsible for collecting taxes and paying pensions or other welfare benefits.

Public services often need massive amounts of money for buildings and staff. The education service and health service are two examples. Until recently, the Government and local authorities used tax payments to finance hospital and school building.

Public services in the UK are usually free when we use them (for example, we do not have to pay when we need hospital treatment). They also serve everyone according to their needs. Sick people use hospitals often but they are not asked to pay more in tax than people who have never needed medical treatment.

Businesses increasingly help to run public services on behalf of the Government and local authorities. They are paid to do this out of the taxes raised by the Government. If the businesses run the services efficiently, they can make a profit out of the arrangement.

 Complete the grid on the right. Place a cross in the correct column to show which public services are provided by local authorities and which by central government. Add two additional public services to the list.

Public service	Central government	Local authorities
The armed forces		
Recycling		
Justice service		
Provision of parks and open spaces		
Building new motorways and trunk roads		
Housing		
Social services		
Health service		
Prison service		

How much responsibility should the state or individuals have for the provision of income protection, health and education?

Businesses have become partners with the Government and local authorities for providing public services such as transport, refuse collection and housing. In these public–private partnerships the money for the service is raised from taxation, collected by the Government or local authority and paid to the company chosen to deliver the service.

All major political parties in the UK approve of public–private partnerships to some extent. Successful partnerships provide good services at a competitive price and make a profit for the business involved. This is possible because the companies involved are experts in their business and can make savings by providing a similar service in several local authority areas. Trade unions have not always been happy with such partnerships because working conditions and pay rates are not always as good as when workers are employed directly by the Government or local authority.

In the future, decisions will need to be made about how far to extend private arrangements into the Government or state's responsibilities for income protection, health and education.

⬆ **A street sweeper at work in Canterbury. Street cleaners and refuse collectors are employed by Serco, an international business. The service is regulated and paid for by Canterbury City Council. This is an example of a successful partnership between a local authority and a business.**

Advantages of direct government (state) provision

- Everyone receives a reasonable service equally.
- People receive a service based on their needs rather than their ability to pay.
- As most people are receiving the same service, standards may be higher than if the state service was only provided for a minority of relatively poor people.
- Elected politicians can maintain close supervision and control of the service.
- Rates of pay and conditions of service for workers in the service are the same across the whole country.

Advantages of private provision

- People can choose the service they want and pay for it accordingly.
- People are encouraged to look ahead and anticipate their needs. This makes them more responsible.
- Business involvement brings in new ideas and drives standards up as companies compete with one another for customers.
- Companies lose business if their service is poor. This encourages them to provide a good service.
- Elected politicians can concentrate on checking service standards and getting good value for the taxpayer.

Education – more private provision?

The Conservative Party is in favour of encouraging more private provision in education. In government, the Labour Party has encouraged businesses, charities and churches to support state education through the Academy Programme. The Conservative Party plans to go further by encouraging groups of parents to start new schools and run them. The purpose of this approach is to provide more choice and improve standards. The whole idea is based on the way the education system is developing in Sweden. There, parents are given a voucher by the government that they can use towards the cost of educating their children in a private school, if they want to do so. If there are no suitable private schools nearby, then groups of parents can set one up. The government's job is to inspect schools to make sure standards are met.

Sample exam questions: Rights and responsibilities as citizens within the economy and welfare systems

Try these questions for the full-course exam (answers on pages 103–105).

5. State one area in which the interests of employers and employees are similar. *(1 mark)*

6. State one way in which the UK Government uses taxation or regulations to encourage environmentally responsible behaviour. *(1 mark)*

7. State one example of a support service that a trade union provides for its members. *(1 mark)*

8. Study Documents 1 and 2 below and overleaf, and answer the questions that follow.

Document 1

Adapted from the BBC News website reporting on the Conservative Party Conference, October 2008

The Conservatives want 'independent state schools', each free to develop their own specialism and ethos.

However, after ten years of Labour government, has that already happened? Schools already have freedom over their budgets. The majority of secondary schools are already specialist schools, academies, or are about to be run by trusts. Parents and other groups already have powers to set up new schools.

So the Conservatives, looking for some clear differences from the Labour Party's policy, have gone for the Swedish Plan. They wish to adopt the plan that gives Swedish parents a voucher that they can use to 'buy' a place at an independent school if they are unhappy with their local state schools. Since then the independent sector in Sweden has grown from educating around 1 per cent of children to 15 per cent.

Document 2

Adapted from the policies of the Conservative, Labour and Liberal Democrat parties in February 2009.

Conservative

Wants to let educational charities, trusts, co-operatives and groups of parents set up new schools in the state sector with state funding.

Wants to spend more on pupils who come from disadvantaged backgrounds, to make sure they get the earliest possible opportunity to choose the best schools and enjoy the best teaching. Also wants to allow smaller schools to be set up to respond to parental demands.

Labour

Committed to the National Challenge – that no school should have fewer than 30 per cent of its pupils achieving five good GCSEs, including in English and maths, by 2011. This ambition would be backed by a £200 million package 2009–2011.

Wants every secondary school to be a Specialist school, a Trust school or an Academy, with a business or university partner for every one of them.

Liberal Democrat

Would take action to make sure that an excellent local school or college serves every community. Would give local authorities a clearer responsibility for school performance, with powers to intervene to improve standards.

Would replace Academies with Sponsor-Managed Schools. This would restore power of local authorities to design and supervise schools.

---

a. State one feature of the Swedish Plan from Document 1. *(1 mark)*

b. State how much Labour would spend on the National Challenge according to Document 2. *(1 mark)*

c. State which political party would give local authorities most responsibility for schools. *(1 mark)*

d. Evaluate the viewpoint that 'it is better for the government and local authorities to provide education, other groups should not be allowed to interfere'. In your answer, you must:
   - Explain arguments in favour of the government and local authorities providing education.
   - Explain arguments in favour of parents, trusts, charities and businesses providing education.
   - Use relevant examples to support your answer.
   - Explain your own point of view. *(6 marks)*

3.3 Extending our understanding of a global citizen's rights and responsibilities

How is sustainable development promoted locally?

What is sustainable development?

In the past twenty years people have begun to understand that we are using up the world's resources too quickly. Our existing way of life is placing an increasing burden on the planet and leading to vast inequalities among the world's people.

The increasing stress we put on **resources** and environmental systems such as water, land and air cannot go on forever. To make matters worse, the world's population continues to increase and already over a billion people cannot meet their basic needs. The aim of sustainable development is to enable all the world's people to enjoy a better quality of life. They should meet their basic needs of food, water, clothing and shelter, without damaging the quality of life for future generations.

Local sustainable development

We all need to change some things about the way we live, if we are to achieve sustainable development. This is particularly true for our everyday actions at home, at school and in the workplace.

At home

In the UK, households are responsible for around 25 per cent of our total carbon emissions. Household energy demand continues to rise, which means we need to act now. Saving energy can save a significant amount of money. Some ways of saving energy are given below:

- Turn off electrical appliances and lights.
- Turn thermostats down.
- Wear warm clothing rather than turning on a heater.
- Shower instead of taking a bath.
- Buy goods with less packaging and that have been made locally.
- Reuse and recycle.
- Insulate your home (grants are available).

At school

Students and teachers have formed green groups in many schools. They have helped to reduce the amount of resources and energy used by the school community. Some schools have installed wind turbines and solar panels so that they can generate power for the community. Below are some ways to save energy at school.

- Walk, cycle or use public transport to and from school.
- Make sure the business manager orders environmentally friendly products such as recycled paper.
- Use the internet for communication rather than paper.
- Reduce, reuse and recycle.

Key terms
Resources Useful naturally occurring substances such as fuels (e.g. coal and oil) and materials (e.g. iron and other metals).

Local Agenda 21

Local Agenda 21 is the local version of the international agreement made at the first United Nations Conference on Environment and Development held in Rio de Janeiro in 1992. The Rio conference (known as the Earth Summit) agreed that changes were necessary to tackle environmental, social and economic problems around the world.

In Rio, 179 countries signed up to the Agenda 21 agreement. More than 1800 local authorities in 64 countries are working on the project. Local authorities in the UK have prepared their own local versions of Agenda 21, designed to reduce waste and improve the environment in their communities. Most Local Agenda 21 plans include recycling schemes, cycle routes, traffic-calming measures, better facilities for pedestrians and advice to the public on being more environmentally friendly.

Implementing Local Agenda 21 is not always easy. For example, people are not always happy to separate their household waste into different containers. For people who live in flats, the storage of these waste containers is difficult. There have also been objections to the change from weekly to fortnightly collections of non-recyclable household waste. In 2009 the demand for recycled paper, plastic and glass fell because of an **economic downturn**. This left local authorities with too little income to pay for their recycling services.

How is sustainable development promoted nationally?

Under the UK Government's sustainable development programme, all government departments must ensure that their actions are environmentally friendly.

The main barriers to success are:

1. **Cost to the public.** In 2000 the Government tried to raise fuel taxes in order to make fuel more expensive and encourage people to use less. They also brought in extra fuel grants for vulnerable groups such as pensioners. There were protests against the tax rises and lorry drivers blockaded oil refinaries so that tankers could not deliver fuel to petrol satations. The Government was forced to abandon the tax increases.

2. **Uncertainty.** The Government wants to encourage the production of fuel-efficient cars, but the car companies will not make these cars on a large scale until they are confident that people will buy them. In the meantime, people are reluctant to buy fuel-efficient cars because the ones on the market are expensive. Car companies could take a risk and start to make the cars in bulk at a reasonable cost, but they would face bankrupcy if the plan failed.

3. **Persuasion takes a long time.** Persuading people to change their behaviour is both time-consuming and expensive. People will do things differently if they receive a bonus payment or free gift. Promising people a brighter future for the next generation does not appeal as strongly as a personal short-term benefit.

Key terms

Carbon emissions The amounts of carbon dioxide produced by industry, transport and everyday activities such as boiling a kettle or having a bath.

Economic downturn When the amount of wealth that a country creates is reduced because of world economic changes.

Department for Communities and Local Government

- Make public spaces cleaner, safer and greener and improve the quality of the built environment in deprived areas.
- Promote sustainable, high-quality design and construction, reduce waste, improve resource efficiency and promote more sustainable buildings.
- Put sustainable development at the heart of the planning system, so that all new buildings must use environmentally friendly materials as well as being energy efficient.

Department of Transport

- Encourage the development of more fuel-efficient vehicles and cleaner fuels.
- Reduce emissions from aircraft.
- Ensure that all schools have a travel plan in place to reduce the number of cars used on the 'school run'.

Department of Culture, Media and Sport

- Support exhibitions on sustainable development.
- Help improve public open spaces.

Department for Environment, Food and Rural Affairs

- Provide international leadership on climate change.
- Promote energy efficiency and get rid of fuel poverty.
- Develop a sustainable food and farming strategy and sustainable fisheries policy.
- Set up an agency for the sustainable management of natural resources at land and sea.

🔑 **Key contributions to sustainable development by government departments.**

How is sustainable development promoted globally?

The United Nations (UN) took the lead in 1992 by holding the Earth Summit in Rio. The leaders of the world met to agree targets for sustainable development and to reduce carbon dioxide emissions. Agenda 21 contains over 2,500 wide-ranging recommendations for action on issues such as:

- reducing wasteful use of natural resources
- fighting poverty
- protecting the atmosphere, oceans and animal and plant life
- promoting sustainable agriculture practices that will feed the world's ever-growing population.

Further summit meetings in Kyoto (1997), Johannesburg (2002) and Bali (2007) reinforced the commitment of the world's governments to promote sustainable development. Ambitious targets were set for cutting **carbon emissions**, reducing poverty, protecting the natural environment and changing people's behaviour.

Is Agenda 21 still relevant?

The UN believes that Agenda 21 remains just as relevant today as it did in 1992. The UN describes the proposals set out in Agenda 21 as realistic and wide-ranging. Communities and businesses have benefited by taking action to implement the proposals. Governments agreed that they did not wish to water down Agenda 21 at the Johannesburg Summit in 2002.

Agenda 21 has been strengthened since 1992. For example, at the UN Millennium Summit in 2000, some 150 world leaders agreed on a range of substantial targets, to be achieved within set time frames. These include cutting by half the proportion of the world's people whose income is less than $1 a day, and the proportion of those who lack access to safe drinking water. However, the USA and Australia withdrew from the agreement. They were worried that reducing carbon emissions would harm industry and threaten jobs because of increased costs.

What progress has been made on the implementation of Agenda 21?

Awareness about sustainable development and Agenda 21 has certainly increased since 1992. There has been progress in negotiating environmental agreements on chemicals, hazardous wastes, bio-safety and climate change, to name a few.

However, there is still a long way to go to get individuals, businesses and governments to take environmental and developmental concerns seriously when they are making decisions. Little has been done to implement the recommendations of Agenda 21 on paying for change in Less Economically Developed Countries (LEDCs) or the sharing of technology.

What are the main barriers to change?

Governments of rich MEDCs (More Economically Developed Countries) and poorer LEDCs (Less Economically Developed Countries) experience different barriers to change:

We need to industrialise if we are to help our people escape from poverty. We must do this quickly and without environmental considerations getting in the way. If we fail, we may face increasing poverty and, possibly, protest from our citizens. The MEDCs have already developed their industries and it is unfair for them to now try to restrict development opportunities for us.

We are having real problems persuading our citizens to reduce energy use. It will be even harder to ask them to cut their standards of living so that people in the LEDCs can have a fairer share of the Earth's resources. They will vote us out at the next election if their standards of living fall. More people need to take Agenda 21 seriously.

What is fair trade?

Businesses based in one country trade with businesses in other countries. When undertaken fairly, trade should lift people out of poverty and improve the quality of lives across the world. However, business pressures and the demand for cheap goods can mean that workers in LEDCs often do not enjoy the basic living standards that most of us in the UK take for granted. Trade should benefit everyone, but unfortunately trade is not evenly balanced.

LEDCs often have only **raw materials** or inexpensive **finished products** to sell. MEDCs are more likely to be selling expensive finished products or complex services such as banking, insurance and communications.

MEDCs often have the power to buy raw materials cheaply but sell finished products and services at a much higher price. This keeps standards of living high in MEDCs but low in LEDCs. Many people see this as an example of unfair trade.

Action has been taken by some governments, pressure groups, businesses and individuals to encourage fair trade. This is where people in the MEDCs agree to pay slightly more for things such as chocolate, coffee, tea, fruit and finished products so that the people who grow and harvest the food or make products get paid properly. Fair trade has helped to raise the standard of living for many people in poorer countries.

The Fairtrade Foundation

Millions of farmers depend on selling their crops to survive, but when prices drop it can spell disaster. If farmers earn less money than it costs to run their farm, they face real hardship, struggling to buy food or keep their children in school. They may even lose their land altogether.

The Fairtrade Foundation helps to make sure that farmers and producer

> ## Key terms
>
> **Raw materials** Things such as cocoa pods, wheat, iron ore and bauxite (aluminium ore) that are grown or mined and can be turned into things that we can eat or use.
>
> **Finished products** Items that we can eat or use, made from raw materials. For example, cocoa pods can be made into chocolate and bauxite can be made into aluminium window frames.

Case Study – Comfort Kumeah from Ghana

Adapted from the Fairtrade Foundation's Fairtrade Schools Action Guide (www.fairtrade.org.uk)

Comfort Kumeah is a widow with five children. As well as farming cocoa beans, Comfort also teaches at her local primary school. She lives in a small town in the Ashanti region of Ghana, and she is a member of Kuapa Kokoo cocoa farmers union, a co-operative with 35,000 members. All the cocoa that Kuapa sells to the Divine Chocolate Company, which makes Divine and Dubble chocolate bars, is Fairtrade. The farmers not only receive a fair price for their cocoa, they also own 45 per cent of the company, which means they enjoy a share of the profits.

'Before, we farmers were cheated, The people who bought from us adjusted the scales and gave us very little money. I joined Kuapa because I saw it was the only organisation which could solve some of our problems – they trade without cheating, with the welfare of farmers at heart.'

'Fairtrade deserves its name because it is fair. We would like more cocoa to be sold to Fairtrade because it means a better price for the producer.'

organisations get a fair and stable price for their products to help them support their families and invest in a better future.

The Fairtrade Foundation is a registered charity that licenses use of the Fairtrade Mark on products in the UK in line with internationally agreed Fairtrade standards. The Foundation was established in 1992 by CAFOD (the Catholic Agency for Overseas Development), Christian Aid, Oxfam, Traidcraft and the World Development Movement.

The Co-operative movement – fair trade in business

The Co-op – Co-operative stores and supermarkets, the Co-operative Bank and Co-operative Insurance – is owned by customers, who join the company as members. Members share the profits and are able to vote on the company's policies. Co-op members have encouraged the company to stock and promote Fairtrade products as part of their ethical food policy.

Co-operative stores and supermarkets have been leading the way on fair trade. Other supermarkets now also stock Fairtrade products and the UK has become the largest fair trade market in the world.

The Co-op was the first major retailer to stock a product carrying the Fairtrade mark when Cafédirect was first sold in Co-op stores in 1994. Next the Co-op brought fair trade bananas to the UK, and in 2000 it became the first retailer to launch an own-brand Fairtrade product – Divine Milk Chocolate.

In 2007 the Co-op launched the UK's first supermarket Fairtrade cotton carrier bag. A donation from the sale of each bag is made to the Wings of Hope children's charity, which provides schooling for poor and orphaned children in India and Malawi. As a result of consulting its members, the Co-op converted all of its own-brand hot drinks to Fairtrade, becoming the first UK retailer to do so. In all, the Co-op stock over 200 different Fairtrade products. The company has also created a £25 million fund to support the development of small businesses in the world's poorest countries.

All this has been good for the Co-op's business. In 2009 the Co-operative Bank was one of only very few banks to increase its profits, as it attracted more business because of its ethical policies.

How can governments encourage fairer trade?

In 2008 the UK Government encouraged the Fairtrade movement by providing £1.2 million over two years to help expand the Fairtrade label internationally.

Launching Fairtrade Fortnight in 2008, the Government's International Development Secretary said, 'UK consumers and businesses recognise the benefits of buying products from developing countries – both in terms of quality and as a simple and effective way of supporting the

Many raw materials and finished products now carry the Fairtrade mark.

poorest people on this earth. Research shows that every two years, UK shoppers have doubled the amount of Fairtrade goods they buy.

'It is also important to remember the bigger trade picture of which Fairtrade labelling is a small but important part. In 2006 UK supermarkets spent around £2.7 billion buying food, clothes and toys from developing countries. We would like to see more British and international retailers stock more products from developing countries — buying Fairtrade-labelled products, and other products made by poor producers.'

The UK Government, as a member of the European Union (EU), is committed to free trade with all other EU nations. This means that businesses from any EU nation can export their products to the UK without any additional tax being added to make the product less attractive to UK consumers.

The EU used to impose high additional taxes (tariffs) on many products from LEDCs to make them more expensive to European consumers. This was so that people would be more likely to buy tax-free goods made by European companies. The EU now imposes very low or zero tariffs on products from LEDCs. By comparison, nearly half of LEDC products exported to the USA and Canada have substantial tariffs imposed on them. This makes trading with these countries difficult for LEDCs.

Free trade (zero tariffs) is good for businesses and workers in LEDCs because they can sell more products overseas. High tariffs are a disadvantage to producers in LEDCs, but they protect businesses and jobs in the richer country. Governments in richer countries have a difficult choice to make and it is always tempting to protect businesses and jobs in your own country, particularly if unemployment is a problem.

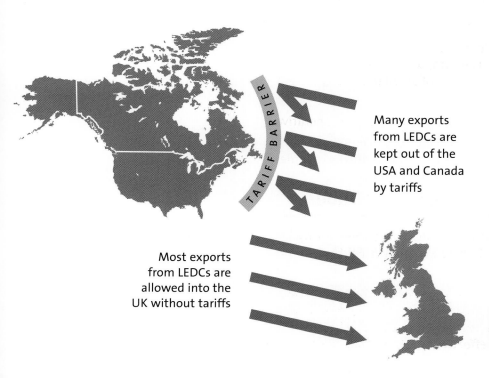

TARIFF BARRIER

Many exports from LEDCs are kept out of the USA and Canada by tariffs

Most exports from LEDCs are allowed into the UK without tariffs

◀ The UK Government encourages fair trade by having few barriers to the import of goods from LEDCs.

Why should MEDCs give aid to LEDCs?

Poverty in LEDCs leads to problems of disease and causes unrest across the world. Around 25 per cent of people worldwide are too poor for a proper diet, good health and a decent education. Many risk their lives trying to move to MEDCs to gain a better standard of living.

Many governments from MEDCs offer support to people in LEDCs. The United Kingdom offers advice, technical support and financial aid to a wide range of other countries, particularly those in the Commonwealth (see page 56). In the event of famine, war or some other disaster in an LEDC, most MEDCs send urgent supplies such as tents, blankets, food and medicines. The United Nations also offers help to people in LEDCs and co-ordinates emergency action where necessary.

Overseas aid can be sent by governments, businesses, charities or individuals. The largest proportion of overseas aid from the UK is sent by the UK Government to governments of LEDCs. However, every year millions of people in the UK raise money to support projects in LEDCs. Much of this is raised through special national events such as Red Nose Day or the BBC Children in Need appeal. Thousands of UK citizens also volunteer to travel to LEDCs to offer their own skills to support development. This is usually done through a charity called Voluntary Service Overseas (VSO).

Table I. Advantages of MEDCs supporting LEDCs

Benefits to the country receiving the aid	Advantages to the country giving the aid
People may be helped to survive when emergency aid is sent.	Richer nations are likely to receive important help and support from the countries to which they are giving aid. This could be military assistance, or support in making links with international organisations or businesses.
Aid helps people meet basic needs of food, water, clothing and shelter. It can support people in their own country and prevent them from becoming refugees.	Governments of countries receiving aid are more likely to encourage businesses to trade with the countries that have helped them.
Aid helps to deal with disease and improve education. It helps people generate wealth more easily and become self-reliant.	Giving aid to people inside their own country helps prevent them trying to emigrate to richer countries.
Aid in the form of machinery, equipment, education or advice can be used by a government directly to support economic growth and development.	Countries that give aid often send equipment and machinery made in their country. This helps to support businesses and create jobs in the country giving the aid.

Case Study: Dr Paul Williams

Until taking up his placement in Africa, Dr Paul Williams was working in a primary care clinic that he opened in 2003 in Stockton-on-Tees (United Kingdom), caring for 600 refugees from 40 countries.

His placement at Bwindi Community Health Centre in Uganda involves training community health workers to provide health care to poorer people in the Batwa and Bakiga communities. Reducing child death rates and treating and caring for HIV and AIDS patients are also high on his agenda. This is very much a hands-on role. Dr Williams' other responsibilities include teaching medical students at the centre, training park rangers in first aid and taking part in the centre's vitally important outreach clinics.

Table J. How effective are different types of overseas aid?

Type and description of aid	Evaluation
Humanitarian aid: Sent quickly in response to an emergency in order to save lives	Giving aid to people in an emergency is always a good thing to do. If we experienced a major problem such as flooding, we would expect help from others to get back on our feet. However, aid can cause problems if the people who receive it come to depend on it too much. For example, wheat was sent to the people of Ethiopia, many of whom were starving. The wheat helped feed the hungry people but the free food drove many Ethiopian farmers out of business because fewer people wanted to buy their millet. This reduced the amount of food Ethiopians were providing for themselves and caused longer-term problems for the people.
Development aid: Designed to fund longer-term projects that aim to help people improve their quality of life	Helping people build their own skills or provide, wells, schools and health centres will lead to people being able to improve their own lives in the longer term. For example, helping people to build a well in a rural community can save them spending two or three hours a day fetching water. The saved time can be used to tend crops or livestock and improve the whole family's quality of life. Development aid works best when it meets people's needs, respects their culture, uses resources within the country and is supported with education and training. It may not be successful if spent on big, unsustainable projects that bring benefits to only a few people.
Bilateral aid: Given by the government of one country directly to another	This can be quick and effective, especially if sent in an emergency. However, bilateral aid is often in the form of equipment and machinery made in the donor country. This may not be exactly what the LEDC needs. Bilateral aid is usually sent directly to an LEDC government, which can then decide how to use it. This gives the LEDC government the power to decide how to use the aid for purposes it sees as being the most important. However, this type of aid is more likely to place the LEDC government in a position where it feels it should support the donor country with diplomatic or military assistance.
Multilateral aid: Given from a fund to which several richer countries contribute; aid from the European Union (EU) or World Bank is multilateral aid	Multilateral aid is more likely to meet the needs of the LEDC and less likely to promote the interests of the country giving the aid. Multilateral aid tends to be aimed at longer-term development projects. Like bilateral aid, it is usually sent to the LEDC government for agreed purposes.
Aid from non-governmental organisations (NGOs): Given by charities such as Oxfam or Save the Children	Charities usually find out exactly what people need in advance and often use local organisations to distribute the aid rather than sending it through a government. This means the aid can be targeted at particular communities and its effects can be evaluated. However, it may also mean that the aid is not co-ordinated or part of any national programme. Some charities have been criticised for using aid to help persuade people to convert to a particular religion.

How does the media affect public opinion?

Websites, newspapers, radio and television (the media) report on the main issues of the day. They search for political scandal and are quick to point out problems. They also give us useful information about important issues and may try to influence our opinions. There are very few limits on what the media can report. This free press is vital in a democracy so that people can find out what politicians are doing (see also page 48).

Nearly all homes in the UK have a radio, TV or the internet; most have all three. Over 50 per cent of the adult population of the UK read a newspaper every day, either by buying one or viewing an online copy. There are ten national daily national newspapers in England. All these newspapers have websites. Web-based news is rapidly gaining importance, as more people prefer to use the internet for their news rather than buy a daily newspaper. Two of the most influential newspapers, *The Times* and *The Sun*, are owned by the same company. Most newspapers support one political party and make this clear to their readers.

Consider the use of emotive language in the examples below and overleaf. What impressions are the writers of the articles trying to communicate to their readers?

Radio and television stations in the UK are required by law to present their news in a fair and balanced way. They are not supposed to favour one political party but are sometimes accused of doing so.

It's a black day for democracy as expenses details are revealed | The Sun |News - Moz

It's a black day for democracy

By GRAEME WILSON
Deputy Political Editor
GARY O'SHEA
and PHILIP CASE
Published: 19 Jun 2009

ADD YOUR COMMENTS

STAGGERING new revelations surrounding MPs' expenses made yesterday the darkest day yet in the amazing Westminster scandal.

The astonishing scale of members' greed, from the Cabinet to back-benchers, was laid bare as details of their claims were published by the Commons.

Amounts ranged from one claim of a single PENNY for a phone call to thousands of pounds for electrical gear.

The figures emerged despite a shameful cover-up which saw pages of claims blacked out by Commons censors.

yourView

FUMING MYSun users have bombarded our website. Here are some of their comments:

Just like the banks, the MPs still have not learned their lessons. Babaza

Government. Whitewash. The two go hand in hand with this lousy lot. Mrs Spratt

Force an election, get out on the streets and demonstrate. Attacotti

This is easy, the ones with the most columns blacked out are the biggest crooks. aufdeutsch

Must try that blacking out on my next tax return, see what happens. Crunchie10

Tell us what you think about the censorship at MYSun

Adapted from The Sun *online (www.thesun.co.uk) June 2009.*

Newspapers and websites use headlines, cartoons and photographs to portray politicians in a certain way. They often slant the news to influence their readers.

PRISON ATTACK EVERY 30 MINUTES

BY JAMES LYONS
11 APRIL 2009

JAILS are 'out of control', with inmates carrying out a violent attack every 30 minutes.

There were 18,929 assaults behind bars last year – more than 50 a day – official figures show.

Violence among adult prisoners is up by almost 50 per cent since 2002 while attacks by young thugs have more than doubled.

And assaults on prison officers in 2008 rose by more than a third in Young Offender Institutions and 14 per cent in adult jails. Lib Dem prison spokesman Paul Holmes, who uncovered the Ministry of Justice figures, warned that criminals risked becoming more violent as a result of time spent in crowded jails.

He said: 'It is completely unacceptable. Our prisons are so out of control that an inmate is able to attack another inmate every half hour.'

Struggling

'This Government's continued obsession with sounding tough on crime has left our prisons packed to the rafters, with prison officers struggling to keep control and themselves safe.'

Adapted from the Mirror newspaper (www.mirror.co.uk) April 2009.

Key terms

Young Offender Institution
Secure accommodation where young offenders aged between 15 and 21 are held in custody.

⬅ **What impression of the Government is created by an article like this?**

Foreign news stations such as CBS and Fox News are not controlled by UK law. They can give their owners' opinions on the big news stories of the day.

How can the media help bring about change in democratic societies?

Imagine a world without TV, the internet, radio and newspapers or magazines. We would need to get our information from personal experience or by 'word of mouth' from other people – friends, family or people at work.

In the nineteenth and early twentieth centuries, people did not have access to the range of media that we now take for granted. Many would go to large political meetings, often in a town square or local park, to hear politicians speak about what they hoped to do if elected. Until 30 years ago, politicians and their supporters would attempt to visit every voter in their home to tell them directly about their policies. Meetings would be held at factory gates, outside schools and in community centres. Today, we get most of our information through the media. We form our opinions of politicians and political parties from what we hear about them over a period of time rather than just when there is an election.

This gives the media considerable power in a democracy. The media can bring about change in a democracy by the following methods:
- Providing information to the public that they might not otherwise know about.
- Asking questions and mounting investigations.
- Exposing mistakes, wrong-doing and corruption.

- Applying pressure on governments to make particular decisions or change the law.
- Supporting or opposing particular viewpoints.
- Supporting or opposing particular political parties.

The BBC *Panorama* programme is just one TV show that investigates important issues, such as the care of the elderly. An investigation by this programme in 2009 exposed problems in the quality of our care for elderly people. *Panorama* used secret filming to expose bad practice by some homecare providers. This investigation led to immediate changes in some of the businesses and local authorities that were investigated.

Britain's homecare scandal

Adapted from the BBC News website (www.bbc.co.uk)

Care of the elderly is a professional job. Assisting medication, feeding, changing, bathing, even using hoists demands a level of expertise we expect in the care of some of our most vulnerable people. But when *Panorama* went undercover in some of Britain's biggest homecare suppliers, we found carers with little more training than they needed for a job in a burger bar.

In democracies, the media safeguards a citizen's right to make informed choices. However, citizens must beware of believing all they read or see in the media.

How can the media help bring about change in non-democratic societies?

Non-democratic societies have always set out to control the media so that news stories and other items reflect well on the government. In many cases the media is not only controlled by the government, but also owned by it. The country's rulers can control the content of books, newspapers, radio and TV. The government censors (cuts or changes) things that it feels might cause people to lose faith in their authority.

Satellite communication is free of censorship and can be accessed anywhere in the world. It is difficult to prevent people communicating freely, receiving international radio and TV stations and using the internet. People can find out new information and exchange ideas without their government being able to stop them. The massive political changes in eastern Europe over the last 30 years, in which non-democratic governments have been overthrown by people demanding change, can be linked to people's greater access to worldwide media such as the BBC's World Service (see above, page 97), and the increasing use of the internet. Put simply, people were able to use the free media to see that their own governments were misleading them.

Non-democratic societies try to use technology and legal restrictions to prevent access to the global media. In China, the government employs 30,000 'cybercops' to monitor internet content. The techniques they have developed for shutting down websites within minutes of them appearing are so refined that China is being approached by countries such as Saudi Arabia, which would like to use similar methods. According to the Committee to Protect Journalists, 18 of the 26 journalists in Chinese prisons in May 2008 worked online. The best known is Shi Tao, a journalist from Changsha, in Hunan province, who was sentenced to ten years in prison for sending an email about media restrictions to an overseas website. He was convicted for 'divulging state secrets abroad'.

While free access to information and opinions from across the world can promote democracy and threaten non-democratic governments, instant worldwide communication can also pose a threat to democracy in several ways.

- Criminals can use uncensored direct access the internet in order to find out about other criminals and identify possible victims.
- Pressure groups can organise illegal action that catches the police off guard.
- Terrorists or extreme, non-democratic political parties can set up websites to publicise their ideas and activities.

Sample exam questions: Extending our understanding of a global citizen's rights and responsibilities

Try these questions for the full-course exam (answers on pages 105–106).

9. State one way in which schools can encourage sustainable development. *(1 mark)*

10. State one advantage to a More Economically Developed Country (MEDC) in giving aid to a Less Economically Developed Country (LEDC). *(1 mark)*

11. State one way in which the media can help bring about change in a democratic society. *(1 mark)*

12. Study Document 1 below and answer the following questions.

    a. State one piece of evidence from Document 1 which shows that not everyone is happy with the Fairtrade scheme. *(1 mark)*

    b. State one reason why the Fairtrade Foundation was happy that Nestlé started selling Fairtrade coffee. *(1 mark)*

    c. State two ways in which fair trade can benefit producers in Less Economically Developed Countries (LEDCs) *(2 marks)*

    d. Evaluate the viewpoint that buying Fairtrade products is the most important thing anyone can do to support people in Less Economically Developed Countries (LEDCs). You must do the following in your answer:

- Explain arguments in favour of the viewpoint that 'buying Fairtrade products is the most important thing anyone can do to support people in LEDCs'.
- Explain arguments against the viewpoint that 'buying Fairtrade products is the most important thing anyone can do to support people in LEDCs'.
- Use relevant examples to support your answer.
- Explain your own point of view. *(6 marks)*

Document 1

Adapted from the BBC website (www.bbc.co.uk)

As the fair trade movement has grown, various questions have been asked.

British Fairtrade. In 2003 farmers in the United Kingdom (UK) asked for Fairtrade certification. In the end, the answer was 'no', because it was felt the scheme should focus on poor farmers in developing countries.

Local versus fair trade. Most Fairtrade food cannot be easily grown in Europe. But since 2003 some Fairtrade products such as apples have been brought from South Africa. The same apples could have been grown in the United Kingdom. Pressure groups are worried about the environmental cost of transporting apples from South Africa to the UK.

The Nestlé debate. In 2005 the company Nestlé started selling Fairtrade coffee. Some people were against this because Nestlé was a company with a poor record on human rights. But the Fairtrade Foundation considered Nestlé's decision a huge success, as it showed that fair trade principles were starting to be taken seriously by big companies.

Section 4 Answers to exam questions

Answers to questions from Section 2: short-course exam

Citizenship, identity and community in the United Kingdom (p.23)

1. What is the best description of an asylum seeker?
(1 mark)

iv. A person wanting refuge and protection.

2. State one reason people in the UK often have a complex sense of identity. *(1 mark)*

One mark for any of the following:

- *A person may find that their childhood religious, cultural or family experience is different from what they experience in later life.*
- *A person may have a mother and father from different cultures or traditions.*
- *A person may experience a conflict between British values and those of their family or ethnic group.*

3. State one example of a British value. (1 mark)

One mark for any of the following: Personal freedom, tolerance, respect for diversity, equal opportunity, democracy and the rule of law.

4. Explain why the United Kingdom is one of the most diverse societies in the world with a wide variety of ethnic groups and languages. In your answer, you should:

- Give suitable examples of the ethnic groups that have settled in the UK.
- Explain why at least two of these ethnic groups came to live in the UK. *(4 marks)*

Level 1. *You should show a limited understanding of what is meant by the terms 'diverse society' and 'ethnic group'. You should show a limited understanding of why this diversity came about with at least one accurate example of a group that has moved to the UK.* *(1–2 marks)*

Level 2. *You should show a sound understanding of what is meant by the terms 'diverse society' and 'ethnic group'. You should show a thorough understanding of how this diversity came about, with accurate examples of groups that have moved to the UK and sound reasons for these migrations.* *(3–4 marks)*

5. Evaluate the following viewpoint: 'Community cohesion is strong in all communities across the United Kingdom.' In your answer, you should :

- Explain what community cohesion is and describe what a cohesive community might be like.
- Describe any communities that lack community cohesion and explain why this might be the case.
- Use evidence or examples to support the points you make.
- Evaluate how far you agree that 'community cohesion is strong in all communities across the United Kingdom'. *(12 marks)*

Level 1. *You should produce a personal response to the statement in which you make some valid but limited points about community cohesion and/or show an understanding of the range of different communities across the UK.* *(1–3 marks)*

Level 2. *You should write some evaluation of the statement, based on some analysis of at least two pieces of valid evidence about the extent of community cohesion in communities across the UK.* *(4–6 marks)*

Level 3. *You should produce a sound personal response to the question, supported by a sound analysis of at least two pieces of valid evidence that show the extent of community cohesion in the UK.* *(7–9 marks)*

Level 4. *You should produce an informed personal response to the question based on a thorough analysis and evaluation of a range of evidence. At this level, your response will contain specific examples of strong community cohesion and the reasons for this strength. You should show that strong community cohesion is not a feature of all communities across the UK, and explain why this is. You should finish your answer with an informed conclusion.* *(10–12 marks)*

Fairness and justice in decision-making and the law (p.36)

6. What is the best description of a Crown Court? *(1 mark)*

iii. A court that deals with serious criminal cases.

7. Give one example of a criminal offence. *(1 mark)*

Any example of an offence against a person's life, health and safety or against their property (theft or damage) or against the state (treason, tax evasion, perjury, obstructing the police, etc.)

8. State one basic rule that governments should follow under international humanitarian law.   *(1 mark)*

    Any one of the following: Not using disproportionate/unreasonable force; protecting civilians; only having military targets; looking after prisoners; etc.

9. Explain why criminal behaviour may threaten human rights. In your answer, you should:
   - Give suitable examples of criminal behaviour to support your answer.
   - Explain which human rights are likely to be under threat as a result of criminal behaviour. *(4 marks)*

    Level 1. *You should show a limited understanding of what is meant by the terms 'criminal behaviour' and 'human rights'. You should show a limited understanding of which human rights may be threatened by criminal behaviour and may, for example, mention the right to life in this context.*
    (1–2 marks)

    Level 2. *You should show a sound understanding of what is meant by the terms 'criminal behaviour' and 'human rights'. You should show a thorough understanding of why human rights are threatened by criminal behaviour and may, for example, point out that in order to combat crime a government may decide to restrict people's right to personal freedom.   (3–4 marks)*

10. Evaluate the following viewpoint: 'The right to privacy must be protected at all costs. There is no more important right than this.' In your answer, you should:
    - Explain why the right to privacy is important and describe how it is protected.
    - Use evidence or examples to support the points you make.
    - Describe other rights that may be equally important or more important than the right to privacy.
    - Evaluate how far you agree that 'there is no more important right' than the right to privacy.
    (12 marks)

    Level 1. *You should produce a personal response to the statement, in which you make some valid but limited points about the right to privacy and may mention other rights.   (1–3 marks)*

    Level 2. *You should write some evaluation of the statement based on some explanation of why the right to privacy is important. You should compare the right to privacy with at least one other right that you have justified as important. (4–6 marks)*

    Level 3. *A sound personal evaluation of the statement supported by a sound explanation why the right to privacy is important with evidence or examples to support your case. You should describe at least two other rights and explain why these are important.   (7–9 marks)*

    Level 4. *An informed personal evaluation of the statement supported by a thorough analysis and evaluation of a range of evidence. At this level, your response will contain specific examples of rights and strong justifications of why they are important. You should show a clear understanding that the right to privacy may compete with other rights and that people's privacy cannot be respected where, for example, they have been involved in a crime. Your answer should end with an informed conclusion.*
    (10–12 marks)

Democracy and voting (p.50)

11. Which description best describes the way in which a representative democracy works?   *(1 mark)*

    iii. *People vote for politicians who then use their judgement to decide how best to run the country.*

12. Give one example of a United Kingdom (UK) political party.   *(1 mark)*

    Any one of: Conservative, Labour, Liberal Democrat (LibDem), Scottish National Party (SNP), Plaid Cymru (Welsh Nationalist Party), Green Party, UK Independence Party (UKIP), Democratic Unionist Party (DUP), Ulster Unionist Party (UUP), Sinn Fein, Social Democratic and Labour Party (SDLP) or any other relevant party in the UK.

13. State one responsibility of the Prime Minister.   *(1 mark)*

    Any one of: Leads his or her political party; chooses ministers/Government; chooses his/her cabinet; liaises with the monarch; calls elections; declares war; leads on important negotiations.

14. Explain why people's human rights are likely to be under threat if they live in a non-democratic country. In your answer, you should:
- Describe the differences between democratic and non-democratic forms of government.
- Explain which human rights are likely to be under threat in a non-democratic country. *(4 marks)*

    Level 1. *You should show a limited understanding of what is meant by the terms 'democracy ' and 'human rights'. You should show a limited understanding of which human rights may be threatened in a non-democratic country and may, for example, mention the right to vote in this context.* *(1–2 marks)*

    Level 2. *You should show a sound understanding of what is meant by the terms 'democracy' and 'human rights'. You should show a thorough understanding of why human rights are threatened in a non-democratic country, giving several informed examples, including such rights as personal freedom, voting, free assembly, standing for election and a fair trial.* *(3–4 marks)*

15. Evaluate the following viewpoint: 'Citizens can gain most influence over decision-making by joining a pressure group.' In your answer, you should:
- Explain why joining a pressure group can help a citizen gain more influence over decision-makers.
- Use evidence or examples to support the points you make.
- Describe other ways in which citizens can gain influence over decision-makers.
- Evaluate how far you agree that joining a pressure group is the way in which a citizen can 'gain more influence over decision-makers'. *(12 marks)*

    Level 1. *You should produce a personal response to the statement in which you make some valid but limited points about why joining a pressure group may help people to gain more influence.* *(1–3 marks)*

    Level 2. *You should write a brief evaluation of the statement based on some explanation of how pressure groups can have more influence than individuals. You should compare membership of pressure groups with at least one other way that citizens might gain influence over decision-makers, such as using the media or joining a political party.* *(4–6 marks)*

Level 3. *You should write a sound personal evaluation of the statement supported by a sound explanation why joining a pressure group can give a person more influence. You should use evidence or examples to support your case. You should describe at least two other ways that citizens can gain influence over decision-makers and explain why these are significant.* *(7–9 marks)*

Level 4. *You should write an informed personal evaluation of the statement supported by a thorough analysis and evaluation of a range of evidence. At this level, your response should contain specific examples of how citizens can increase their influence by joining pressure groups or otherwise, and of how pressure groups work. You should finish your answer with an informed conclusion.* *(10–12 marks)*

There is a model answer to this question on page 106.

The UK and the wider world (p.60)

16. Which two countries [in list below] are members of the Commonwealth? *(1 mark)*

    i. Canada and iv. South Africa.

17. State one aim of the European Union (EU). *(1 mark)*

    Any one of: free trade; gain strength through partnership; spread democracy; promote human rights; harmonisation of laws, regulations, etc; promote co-operation and joint projects; support weaker regions.

18. State one way in which the United Nations (UN) tries to resolve conflict. *(1 mark)*

    Any one of: Promoting international agreements, treaties and laws; using the International Court of Justice; using sanctions, sending a peacekeeping mission.

19. Explain why some people might think that the United Kingdom (UK) should stop being a member of the European Union (EU). In your answer, you should:
- Give examples of the disadvantages of EU membership.
- Explain why people might feel strongly about at least one of these disadvantages. *(4 marks)*

    Level 1. *You should show a limited understanding of what is meant by the European Union and its significance for the United Kingdom. You should* *show a limited understanding of disadvantages of membership and may, for example, mention loss of control in this context.* *(1–2 marks)*

Level 2. *You should show a sound understanding of what is meant by the European Union. You should show a thorough understanding of the consequences of EU membership for the UK and explain why people may feel strongly about them. In this context you should discuss at least two disadvantages such as cost, delay/lack of flexibility, loss of sovereignty or the lack of focus on potentially stronger trading links.* *(3–4 marks)*

20. Evaluate the following viewpoint: 'The United Nations (UN) is a waste of money.' In your answer, you should:

- Explain why the UN was set up.
- Describe what the UN does.
- Use evidence or examples to support the points you make.
- Evaluate how far you agree that 'the UN is a waste of money'. *(12 marks)*

Level 1. *You should produce a personal response to the statement in which you make some valid but limited points about what the UN does and/or why it was set up.* *(1–3 marks)*

Level 2. *You should write a brief evaluation of the statement based on some explanation of what the UN does and why it was set up. This may include such points as emergency relief and peacekeeping missions. You should use some examples to support your points.* *(4–6 marks)*

Level 3. *You should write a sound personal evaluation of the statement supported by a sound explanation why the UN was set up and what it does. You should use evidence or examples to support your case. These include a more comprehensive consideration of the work of the UN on promoting human rights, education and international law.* *(7–9 marks)*

Level 4. *You should write an informed personal evaluation of the statement supported by a thorough analysis and evaluation of a range of evidence. At this level, your response should contain specific examples of what the UN does and the value or otherwise of its work. You should have an informed conclusion to your answer. (10–12 marks)*

Answers to questions from Section 3: full-course exam

Answer to Activity on page 63: All the examples are legal rights.

Rights and responsibilities in school, college and the wider community (p.72)

1. State one way in which rights are reinforced in schools. *(1 mark)*

   Any one of the following: Through school policies or school rules; through a Home–School agreement; through the use of rewards or punishments; through the legal system.

2. State one legal responsibility of teacher in a school. *(1 mark)*

   To act as careful parents would towards their own children of a similar age.

3. State three different rights that parents have if they have school-age children. *(3 marks)*

   Any three of the following: choose a school for their children; appeal against a local authority's allocation of a school place; educate their children at home; withdraw their child from sex education lessons; see their child's school records; appeal against a decision to exclude their child from school; receive at least one progress report each year.

4. Study Document 1 overleaf and answer the following questions.

a. State one piece of evidence from Document 1 that shows that staff training was a problem for Redbridge Council. *(1 mark)*

b. State two ways in which Mr Bennett's complaint has been put right. *(2 marks)*

c. Write a reasoned argument to oppose the viewpoint that 'complaining about the actions of organisations that provide public services is difficult and usually a waste of time'. You must do the following in your answer:
   - Explain key terms such as public services.
   - Explain how a complaints process works.
   - Use evidence to support your argument.
   (6 marks)

Document 1. Ombudsman criticises Council over disabled homeless applicant

Adapted from the website of the Local Government Ombudsman (www.lgo.org.uk)

The London Borough of Redbridge failed to take sufficient account of a man's hearing disability when dealing with his homelessness application, finds Local Government Ombudsman Tony Redmond.

The Ombudsman finds that the Council was at fault for several reasons, including:

- Interviewing Mr Bennett without a British Sign Language (BSL) interpreter even though he cannot communicate without a BSL interpreter.
- Delaying unreasonably for 12 months the promised training for frontline staff on disability awareness.
- Failing to comply with the requirements of the Disability Discrimination Act to make 'reasonable adjustments' to enable disabled people to access services.

The Council has already paid Mr Bennett £750 for failing to provide an interpreter and a textphone facility. Council staff have now had Deaf Awareness Training and a textphone facility has been provided. In addition, the Ombudsman also considers that the Council should:

- Pay Mr Bennett an additional £500 for the inconvenience.
- Remind all staff of the importance of recording service users' special communication needs and checking these records before attempting to contact them.
- Remind all staff of the importance of complying with its Interpretation and translation policy.

a. *Any one of the following: The council failed to take account of Mr Bennett's disability; Mr Bennett was interviewed without an interpreter; training was delayed for twelve months; the staff have now had deaf awareness training; the recommendations about 'reminding staff'.*

b. *Any two of the following: He has been paid compensation; the staff have been trained; the staff have been reminded; a textphone facility has been installed.*

c. **Level 1**. *You should write a personal response to the viewpoint in which you show a limited understanding of the term 'public services'.*

Information is organised at a limited level to aid communication. For two marks, you also give at least one piece of evidence to support your argument. (1–2 marks)

Level 2. *You should write a sound personal response to the viewpoint in which you use evidence to oppose it. You clearly understand the term 'public services' and support this understanding with examples. Text is legible, and spelling, grammar and punctuation are mostly accurate. Meaning should be communicated clearly.* (3–4 marks)

Level 3. *As for level 2 above. In addition you offer an informed personal response to the viewpoint in which you show a thorough understanding of how a complaints process works.* (5–6 marks)

Rights and responsibilities as citizens within the economy and welfare systems (p.83)

5. State one area in which the interests of employers and employees are similar. (1 mark)

Any one of the following: Ensure that the business is successful; make sure workers are well-motivated; ensure that health and safety is in place; ensure good staff training; deal with any workplace problems efficiently; ensure good management.

6. State one way in which the United Kingdom (UK) Government uses taxation or regulations to encourage environmentally responsible behaviour. (1 mark)

Any one of the following: Putting fuel duty on petrol/diesel; carbon tax; landfill tax; graduated road tax (on CO_2 emissions); congestion charging; scrappage allowance; grants for energy efficiency; regulations on pollution; home energy reports; energy reports on electrical appliances such as fridges and cookers.

7. State one example of a support service that a trade union provides for its members. (1 mark)

Any one of the following: Legal advice and support; help line; local representative; representation with the employer; pay negotiations; negotiation on working conditions; support on health and safety matters; discounts; insurance; pensions advice; benevolent service; support and advice to family in the event of death or injury.

8. Study Documents 1 and 2 below and answer the questions that follow.

a. State one feature of the Swedish Plan from Document 1. *(1 mark)*

b. State how much Labour would spend on the National Challenge according to Document 2. *(1 mark)*

c. State which political party would give local authorities most responsibility for schools. *(1 mark)*

d. Evaluate the viewpoint that 'it is better for the government and local authorities to provide education, other groups should not be allowed to interfere'. In your answer, you must do the following.
- Explain arguments in favour of the government and local authorities providing education.
- Explain arguments in favour of parents, trusts, charities and businesses providing education.
- Use relevant examples to support your answer.
- Explain your own point of view. *(6 marks)*

Document 1

Adapted from the BBC News website reporting on the Conservative Party conference, October 2008

The Conservatives want 'independent state schools', each free to develop their own specialism and ethos.

However, after ten years of Labour government, has that already happened? Schools already have freedom over their budgets. The majority of secondary schools are already specialist schools, academies, or are about to be run by trusts. Parents and other groups already have powers to set up new schools.

So the Conservatives, looking for some clear differences from the Labour Party's policy, have gone for the Swedish Plan. They wish to adopt the plan that gives Swedish parents a voucher that they can use to 'buy' a place at an independent school if they are unhappy with their local state schools. Since then the independent sector in Sweden has grown from educating around one per cent of children to fifteen per cent.

Document 2

Adapted from the policies of the Conservative, Labour and Liberal Democrat parties in February 2009.

Conservative

Wants to let educational charities, trusts, co-operatives and groups of parents set up new schools in the state sector with state funding.

Wants to spend more on pupils who come from disadvantaged backgrounds, to make sure they get the earliest possible opportunity to choose the best schools and enjoy the best teaching. Also wants to allow smaller schools to be set up to respond to parental demands.

Labour

Committed to the National Challenge – that no school should have fewer than 30 per cent of its pupils achieving five good GCSEs, including in English and maths, by 2011. This ambition would be backed by a £200 million package 2009–2011.

Wants every secondary school to be a Specialist school, a Trust school or an Academy, with a business or university partner for every one of them.

Liberal Democrat

Would take action to make sure that an excellent local school or college serves every community. Would give local authorities a clearer responsibility for school performance, with powers to intervene to improve standards.

Would replace Academies with Sponsor-Managed Schools. This would restore power of local authorities to design and supervise schools.

a. *Parents are given a voucher or they can spend it at an independent school.*

b. *£200 million.*

c. *The Liberal Democrats.*

d. **Level 1**. *This should be a personal response to the viewpoint in which you show a limited understanding of the alternative ways in which education can be provided. Information is organised at a limited level to aid communication. For two marks, you should also give at least one relevant example to support your argument.* *(1–2 marks)*

Level 2. *You should write a sound personal response to the viewpoint in which you make points on both sides of the argument. You should* clearly understand the alternative ways in which education can be provided and support this understanding with examples. Text must be legible, and spelling grammar and punctuation should be mostly accurate. Meaning should be communicated clearly. *(3–4 marks)*

Level 3. As for Level 2 above. In addition you offer an informed personal response to the viewpoint in which you show a thorough understanding of the arguments on both sides of the case. (5–6 marks)

Extending our understanding of a global citizen's rights and responsibilities (p. 97)

9. State one way in which schools can encourage sustainable development. *(1 mark)*

Any one of the following: Starting a green group; saving energy; buying environmentally friendly products; modifying the curriculum to include more opportunity for learning about sustainability; having a travel plan; installing solar/wind generation; reduce; reuse; recycle.

10. State one advantage to a More Economically Developed Country (MEDC) in giving aid to a Less Economically Developed Country (LEDC). *(1 mark)*

Any one of the following: Any valid humanitarian reason (it's the right thing to do); to gain military advantage; to gain a trading partner; to create business / jobs in its own country; to gain diplomatic advantage.

11. State one way in which the media can help bring about change in a democratic society. *(1 mark)*

Any one of the following: Influence decision-makers; provide information to the public; persuade the public; expose wrong-doing; scrutinise political policies/ actions; organise or support campaigns.

12. Study Document 1 and answer the following questions.

a. State one piece of evidence from Document 1 that shows that not everyone is happy with the Fairtrade scheme. *(1 mark)*

b. State one reason why the Fairtrade Foundation was happy that Nestlé started selling Fairtrade coffee. *(1 mark)*

c. State two ways in which fair trade can benefit producers in Less Economically Developed Countries (LEDCs). *(2 marks)*

d. Evaluate the viewpoint that buying Fairtrade products is the most important thing anyone can do to support people in Less Economically Developed Countries (LEDCs). You must do the following in your answer:

● Explain arguments in favour of the viewpoint that 'buying Fairtrade products is the most important thing anyone can do to support people in LEDCs'.

● Explain arguments against the viewpoint that 'buying Fairtrade products is the most important thing anyone can do to support people in LEDCs'.

● Use relevant examples to support your answer.

● Explain your own point of view. *(6 marks)*

Document 1

Adapted from the BBC website (www.bbc.co.uk)

As the fair trade movement has grown, various questions have been asked.

British Fairtrade. In 2003 farmers in the United Kingdom (UK) asked for Fairtrade certification. In the end, the answer was 'no', because it was felt the scheme should focus on poor farmers in developing countries.

Local versus fair trade. Most Fairtrade food cannot be easily grown in Europe. But since 2003 some Fairtrade products such as apples have been brought from South Africa. The same apples could have been grown in the United Kingdom. Pressure groups are worried about the environmental cost of transporting apples from South Africa to the UK.

The Nestlé debate. In 2005, the company Nestlé started selling Fairtrade coffee. Some people were against this because Nestlé was a company with a poor record on human rights. But the Fairtrade Foundation considered Nestlé's decision a huge success, as it showed that fair trade principles were starting to be taken seriously by big companies.

---

a. *Any one of: Excluding British farmers; environmental costs not taken into account (or similar); giving Fairtrade certification to 'big companies'/Nestlé.*

b. *It showed that fair trade principles were starting to be taken seriously by big companies (or similar).*

c. *Any two of: They are paid a fair price; they are paid a stable price; farmers are encouraged to co-operate; they have a say in the business; there is training; there are health benefits; there is more money to invest in the community.*

d. **Level 1**. *You should write a personal response to the viewpoint in which you show a limited understanding of the benefits of buying Fairtrade products and/or of the alternative actions that might support people in LEDCs, such as campaigning; setting up exchanges; investment; environmental measures; free trade; education, etc. Information is organised at a limited level to aid communication. For two marks, you also give at least one relevant example to support your argument. (1–2 marks)*

Level 2. *You should write a sound personal response to the viewpoint in which you make* points on both sides of the argument. You should show that you clearly understand alternative ways in which people in LEDCs can be supported and back up this understanding with examples. Text is legible, and spelling grammar and punctuation are mostly accurate. Meaning is communicated clearly. (3–4 marks)

Level 3. *As for level 2 above. In addition you should offer an informed personal response to the viewpoint in which you show a thorough understanding of the arguments on both sides of the case.* (5–6 marks)

A model answer for the essay in the short-course exam

> **Evaluate the following viewpoint: 'Citizens can gain most influence over decision-making by joining a pressure group.'**
>
> There is no doubt that a pressure group can usually have more influence over government policy than someone acting on his or her own. So if you have a particular point to make, use the internet to find a pressure group that represents that viewpoint. By making the pressure group bigger and, more importantly, helping with their campaigns, you can add to their influence.
>
> A pressure group such as Greenpeace, Amnesty or the RSPCA will already have contacts with MPs and civil servants. In fact, government officials may consult leading members of the group when a new law is being considered. A pressure group will have its own website and good contacts with people in the media who will be happy to publish the group's press releases.
>
> The RSPCA has a good record of success in persuading governments to change laws to benefit animals. For example, the RSPCA lobbied the Government in the consultation stages on the recent Animal Act and obtained important changes to the new law.
>
> There are other ways in which you can gain influence over decision-makers. For example, you could start a blog or write an article for the press as part of a campaign. This helps to get your voice heard. One man started Amnesty by making an appeal in a newspaper. Other people saw the article and got in touch. A pressure group was born. This again, supports the point that pressure groups have an important part to play in a democracy.
>
> All politicians are members of a political party. Anyone can join a party and each one has local branches that hold meetings and discussions. You can even put forward your own ideas for policies in the hope that other party members might agree with you. Each year, the political parties have conferences at which these ideas are discussed. The political party then puts forward the agreed ideas at election time in their manifesto.
>
> In conclusion, pressure groups do enable citizens to gain more influence over decision makers. This is usually over single issues or particular areas of policy. On the other hand, political parties consider all areas of policy. If you can find a party that agrees with you, then you could join to give yourself even more influence.

← Strong opening statement that is relevant to the question

← Point made clearly with examples of pressure groups and how they influence decision-makers.

← Point backed up with specific evidence.

← First point made about other ways to influence decision-makers.
← Point backed up with specific evidence.
← Reference back to the question.
← Second point made about other ways to influence decision-makers.
← Point backed up with evidence but lacking specific examples this time.

← Clear and final evaluation of the viewpoint.

Section 5 Glossary of key terms

Abortion
The termination (ending) of a pregnancy at an early stage, usually through a surgical operation.

Act (of Parliament)
A Bill (a new law) that has been approved by Parliament becomes a statute law, and is known as an Act of Parliament.

Asylum seeker
A person seeking political asylum (safety) in another country.

Authority
Having the right to use power.

BBC (British Broadcasting Corporation)
The UK's publicly owned broadcasting company. It is regulated by a Royal Charter. This sets out its responsibilities to be impartial and also to inform, educate and entertain the public.

Bill
The name given to a proposed new law as it passes through Parliament.

Blog
A type of website, usually maintained by one person with regular entries of commentary, descriptions of events, or other material such as graphics or video.

Cabinet
The Prime Minister and the senior MPs he or she has chosen to help run the country. There are usually around twenty people in the Cabinet.

Candidate
A person who asks people to vote for him/her as their representative.

Carbon emissions
The amounts of carbon dioxide produced by human activities.

Civil servant
A professional administrator employed by the state (the country) to carry out tasks given to them by the government. Civil servants should not support a particular political party. They put new laws into operation and carry out government policies. For example, politicians could decide to build a new university, but civil servants would be responsible for actually making it happen.

Classical democracy
A form of democracy in which citizens vote frequently and directly on issues of the day.

Community cohesion
People sharing a sense of belonging and community identity.

Colonising
Conquering and taking over the control of a region or country.

Compensation
A sum of money paid in return for any loss or damage someone has suffered.

Constituency
An area of the country with around 60,000 voters. Each of the 646 constituencies in the UK elects one MP to Parliament.

Council of Europe
An organisation of more than 40 European states, founded in 1949, which protects human rights through international agreement. It should not be confused with the European Council, which is a policy-making body of the EU.

Crown
The state or government. In the UK, the King or Queen is the head of the state or government. This is why the term 'Crown' is used.

Crown Court
The court used by the state or government for trials of serious criminal offences.

Crown Prosecution Service (CPS)
The CPS considers the information provided by the police about the activities of alleged criminals. The CPS decides whether there is enough evidence to take the matter to court and whether to do so would be in the public interest.

Damages
Money awarded by a court to compensate someone for the loss or injury they have suffered.

Democracy
A system of government in which decisions are taken either by the population directly or through representatives they have elected.

Economic development
Building up a country's ability to produce things that other people want to buy.

Economic downturn
When the amount of wealth that a country creates is reduced because of world economic changes.

Empire
A group of countries under the rule of a single person or state. In the British Empire, for example, Canada, India and large parts of Africa were ruled from London.

European Court of Human Rights (ECtHR)
A court that decides on cases in which it is claimed there has been a breach of the European Convention on Human Rights.

Euthanasia	The process of helping someone to die in a dignified way before they would normally do so.
Finished products	Items that we can eat or use, made from raw materials. For example, cocoa pods can be made into chocolate and bauxite can be made into aluminium window frames.
Formal action	This is an action that is part of a legal process and is carefully recorded. The exclusion of a student from school is an example of formal action. There are strict national guidelines that head teachers have to follow. Parents have the right to ask school governors to review any decision.
Free press	Newspapers, TV, radio and other media that are not controlled by a government. The free press can publish anything as long as it is not damaging to individuals and does not encourage people to break the law.
General election	An election to choose the MPs who will form a new Parliament. A general election is held at least once every five years.
High Court	The court that deals with the most important and high value cases in England and Wales.
Home–school agreement	A written agreement that sets out the rights and responsibilities of teachers, students and parents in a school or college.
House of Commons	The 646 democratically elected MPs form the House of Commons.
House of Lords	Members of the House of Lords (peers) either inherit their position or are chosen for their wisdom by the leaders of the main political parties. Peers debate new laws and offer their advice on possible changes.
Immigrant	A person who has left their home region or country and is living in another region or country.
Informal action	This type of action is not placed on any record and usually will not involve any legal process. School governors, police or lawyers are unlikely to be involved. A break-time detention or a parent emailing a teacher to complain that work has not been marked are examples of informal action.
International Court of Justice	Also known as the World Court, the International Court of Justice was set up by the United Nations to settle legal disputes between countries so as to avoid conflict between them.
International humanitarian law	A set of rules that aims to protect people's rights in wartime. It protects people who are not or are no longer fighting. It also places limits on the weapons and tactics that can be used in war.
Judge	A legally trained and experienced lawyer who keeps order during a trial, advises the jury and decides sentences.
Jury	A group of ordinary people aged eighteen and over. In a Crown Court the jury decides whether an accused person is guilty or not guilty.
Legal rights	Expectations that the law says must be met. For example, we expect to be educated in a safe classroom. This is a legal right. If we are injured because a classroom is unsafe, we have a legal right to compensation.
Libellous	A piece of writing or broadcasting that is untrue and could damage someone's reputation.
Licence fee	The BBC is paid for directly through a fee paid by each household for any electronic device used for receiving TV programmes. This allows the BBC to run a wide range of popular public services for everyone without adverts and independent from the influence of advertisers, shareholders or politicians.
Magistrates Court	A court through which all criminal cases pass. Serious cases are sent to the Crown Court for trial. Some minor criminal matters are tried in the Magistrates Court, which also grants licences for the sale of alcohol and other potentially controversial local matters.

Manifesto	A document produced by a political party before an election, which sets out for voters what the party promises to do if it gets into power.	**Political party**	A group of people with similar views who form an organisation to get its members elected to government (either local or national).
Maternity leave	Paid leave from work for female workers who are expecting a baby. In 2009, 39 weeks of leave was granted for each pregnancy.	**Policy**	A statement about what a political party will do on an issue, such as education, health care or taxation, when it gets into power.
Media	Newspapers, TV, the internet and any other means of communicating ideas or information.	**Power**	Making decisions that affect others.
Moral responsibilities	What we should do to support others so that they can enjoy certain rights. For example, students have a responsibility to make sure that their behaviour does not interfere with others' right to learn.	**Press release**	Businesses, celebrities, politicians, pressure groups and charities write their own accounts of events or set out their opinions on an issue. They send this to newspapers, broadcasters and websites for publication.
Moral rights	What we expect from others in certain contexts. For example, parents expect to be contacted by teachers if their son or daughter misbehaves. This is not a legal right but parents still expect it to happen. Therefore it is a moral right — based on what can be reasonably expected in a school context.	**Pressure group**	A group of people with similar views on a single issue who lobby elected representatives.
		Prime Minister	The Prime Minister is leader of one of the political parties in Parliament — usually the party with the most MPs. He or she is asked by the Queen to select the Government to run the country.
National minimum wage	As long as they are aged sixteen or over, workers have the right to receive pay per hour at a rate set by the Government or higher. In 2009 the minimum hourly rate for a sixteen-year-old was £3.53 per hour.	**Raw materials**	Things such as cocoa pods, wheat, iron ore and bauxite (aluminium ore) that are grown or mined and can be turned into things that we can eat or use.
Ombudsman	An ombudsman checks to see whether people have been treated unfairly by looking into complaints about services they have used such as the National Health Service.	**Referendum**	A vote on a single issue in which all citizens can take part.
		Register of Electors	A list of those people who can vote in an election.
Parliament	The main law-making body of the United Kingdom, consisting of the House of Commons, the House of Lords and the Crown (the king or queen).	**Representative democracy**	A form of democracy in which citizens choose representatives, who vote on issues and do their best to represent the other citizens.
Paternity leave	Paid leave from work for the partner of a women who gives birth. In 2009 workers had a right to two weeks' leave.	**Resources**	Useful naturally occurring substances such as fuels (e.g. coal and oil) and materials (e.g. iron and other metals).
		Retailing	Buying and selling. A retail business is a shop or other outlet for selling goods (for example an online bookseller).
Peacekeeping mission	An attempt by a country or group of countries, such as the United Nations, to send armed forces to another country to prevent fighting and settle a dispute.	**Sanctions**	Penalties that are imposed on a country by other countries in order to encourage that country to change its policies. For example, Commonwealth countries cut their trade with Zimbabwe to encourage its government to extend human rights.

School governor — School governors have responsibility for choosing a head teacher, deciding school policies and making sure the school has high standards. Parents, teachers, students and others such as local business people can become school governors.

UK Border Agency — The public body responsible for dealing with asylum and immigration.

United Nations (UN) — An international organisation to which most countries of the world belong. It aims to promote peace, prevent war and maintain world security.

UN Charter — A charter is a document that sets out the purpose of an organisation and the rights it expects members to promote. The UN Charter on Human Rights sets out the human rights that member countries are expected to follow.

UN General Assembly — A meeting of all the member countries of the United Nations. It decides the policies and budget of the United Nations as well as appointing the non-permanent members to the Security Council.

UN Security Council — The UN body that carries out the policy of the General Assembly by maintaining international peace and security. The Security Council can start peacekeeping operations, impose sanctions and organise military action.

Values — Beliefs or principles that we hold to be important.

Young Offender Institution — Secure accommodation where young offenders aged between 15 and 21 are held in custody.

Youth Court — A court where young people under eighteen are tried for criminal offences. Trials are conducted less formally than in an adult court and may not be reported in the media.